FROM BULLET TO BULLHORN

STORIES OF ADVOCACY, ACTIVISM AND HOPE

LOIS A. SCHAFFER

From Bullet to Bullhorn

Copyright © 2021 Lois A. Schaffer

All rights reserved.

Published by Red Penguin Books

Bellerose Village, New York

No part of this book may be reproduced in any form or by any electronic or mechanical means, including information storage and retrieval systems, without written permission from the author, except for the use of brief quotations in a book review.

For Susan Schaffer: Her vitality, spirit and our love live on

AND

to the memory of the victims included within these pages, all victims of gun violence whose losses were tragic and deeply mourned.

IN PRAISE FOR "FROM BULLET TO BULLHORN"

"The Holocaust was always an appalling tragedy in my consciousness, but it was only when I began to interview survivors did the horror of that period become compelling. They were human beings, mother, fathers, sisters and brothers. Schaffer's book brilliant forces the reader to face the gut-wrenching reality that the stories are about real people. Her own experience has created a profound ability to show the reality of what gun violence does daily in America. This book is not anti-gun but rather a pro-human cry to create a culture that values life more than the unbridled love of guns."

S.J. Tagliareni, Former Catholic Priest, business consultant and author: *Hitler's Priest, The Cross or the Swastika, The Architect of Auschwitz, On the Corner and Roving Leadership*

"This is Lois Schaffer's second book about gun violence in the U.S. and the devastating and long-lasting impacts on families. I have known Lois for many years and have always *admired her willingness to speak truth to power, despite the inconceivable pain she experiences from the loss of her daughter, Susie, to gun violence. 'From Bullet to Bullhorn' chronicles the important stories of 18 people who lost loved ones to gun violence. While each story is unique, they unfortunately weave a common thread crying out for necessary change."*

Andy Pelosi, Executive Director, The Campaign to Keep Guns Off Campus

---

"Lois Schaffer's poignant book is a compilation of personal stories written by people who know the exquisite pain of losing a loved one to gun violence. Each story conveys their respective transformation to becoming a warrior in a battle that is uniquely American, that is, to reduce gun violence. Now, if only America would listen."

Michelle Schimel is a former New York State representative whose signature issue is gun violence prevention (GVP). She serves on the executive board of New Yorkers Against Gun Violence.

"Policies in my state and our nation ignore the link between easy access to guns and the act of violence that quashes a human life and leaves survivors' lives forever changed. 'From Bullet to Bullhorn' shares the devastating reality of death by gun violence through heart-wrenching real stories that bring the shock, the pain, the holes in the heart that also irrevocably change the lives of the survivors. The book brings to life the stories of death that otherwise

have become so common that a 'sending thoughts and prayers' response allow those unaffected to go back to their lives ... until the next ubiquitous and senseless attack touches the previously untouched. Share the stories, work for policies, and vote for those who share your voice."

Hon. Jill Schupp, Missouri Senator, District 24

(pronouns: she/her)

"'From Bullet to Bullhorn' is a powerful testimony to human resilience. Each chapter reveals courageous strength and spiritual fortitude as told by those who lost the physical presence of loved ones only to convert that presence into a unique gift of determination to live life with meaning. I couldn't put it down and each chapter (each family's story) revealed human strength beyond one's imagination."

Bennett F. Miller, Rabbi Emeritus, Anshe Emeth Memorial Temple, New Brunswick, New Jersey, National Chair, ARZA

"'From Bullet to Bullhorn' transcends beyond a gripping tragedy to a blueprint for transformational healing advocacy. Lois Schaffer's testimony should be required reading for survivors and proponents of restorative justice."

Rev. Rodrick Burton, Pastor of New Northside Missionary Baptist Church, St. Louis, Missouri

"Reading 'From Bullet to Bullhorn' took me back to my post-med residency training in the Bronx, New York. I saw people on the best days of their lives, as they delivered their babies and, on the worst, as their loved ones died in front of them. Many deaths we cannot prevent even as medicine progresses. But it's the needless deaths that gnaw at me. The Bronx had gangs, and on most shifts, there were numerous trauma alerts for gunshot and stab wounds. Many of those traumas then led to discussions of organ donations with parents of brain-dead teenagers. Now, as a wife and mother, of three young children, I pray that my kids grow up in a world without the threat of gun violence."

Pamela D. Portnoy-Saitta, DO

Emergency Medicine Attending Physician

"'From Bullet to Bullhorn' is an inspiring hope filled book about the resilience of the human spirit. This is a compilation of powerful stories about individuals who despite being impacted by gun violence, refuse to be victims, and instead turn their tragedy into activism and advocacy. Reading this will give anyone who has had a loss hope that not only can you survive, but you can eventually thrive, and go on to create change in profound ways."

Dr. Heidi Horsley, Executive Director, Open to Hope Foundation, Author of Award-Winning Open to Hope book series, Columbia University: Adjunct Professor

"Sometimes those who make the biggest impact on our lives are citizens touched by tragedy. Lois has taken the most unimaginable tragedy and turned her grief into activism. Heartache into action. I've never met another human like Lois, but unfortunately, she is she is not alone. So many in our country have been impacted by gun violence, and Lois has worked tirelessly to make sure some of the stories of her fellow survivors are told. Thank you, Lois for all the work you do...and though she be little, she is fierce."

Hon. Gina Sillitti, New York State Assemblymember, Nassau County, 16th District

"What will it take to newly sensitize average Americans to the horror of gun violence, reacquaint them with the brutality of small boys and girls being slaughtered in their classrooms? The latest literary offering of Lois A. Schaffer, who lost a child to gun violence, is an attempt to bring the stories home and, yes, make them personally painful, because something must shake America from the mental miasma that has normalized kindergarten shooter drills. Schaffer's 'From Bullet to Bullhorn' is not an easy book to read, nor should it be."

Dr. Robert S. Widom, Rabbi, Temple Emanuel, Great Neck, New York

"Lois Schaffer's poignant and fearless advocacy for gun safety in America is illuminated through the wrenching stories of loss and healing chronicled in 'From Bullet to Bullhorn.' I am truly in awe of the courage shown by the families and

loved ones who opened their hearts with the hope of helping others. May the words on these pages be a catalyst for the changes we need to end our nation's epidemic of gun violence once and for all."

Nassau County Legislature Minority Leader Kevan Abrahams, Legislator, District 1

"After enduring a loss that no parent ever should bear, Lois Schaffer has channeled her family's pain into tenacious advocacy for stronger gun safety laws. Her courage is a beacon of hope. Her determination is a source of personal inspiration for anyone who is grappling with loss in their lives. As an elected official, I continue to push for laws and programs that will end the scourge of gun violence in our society."

Hon. Siela A. Bynoe, Nassau County Legislator, District 2

"In today's world, truth is being challenged, and falsehoods are providing easy access to escape empiricism. ("Hallelujah") In 'From Bullet to Bullhorn' we are introduced to survivors in real time. Surviving heroes honoring the memories of their loved ones with herculean vigilance. Each essay provides us with riveting and provocative narrations putting a human face on the victims and each essay is very descriptive of their perseverance while living with their daily pain. Lois Schaffer exhorts the community's conscience to challenge all to advocate for change, whether directly or indirectly stained by it."

Bernice Sims, LCSW, Author "Detour Before Midnight: Freedom Summer Memoirs: James Chaney, Andrew Goodman and Michael Schwerner.

"I was pulled into every chapter of 'From Bullet to Bullhorn.' It is a compelling and carefully curated collection of personal stories, each shared by individuals directly impacted by gun violence. While sometimes deeply disturbing, their accounts are both educational and eye opening. It is my hope that these captivating stories of grief, engagement and activism will help readers recognize the need to change the culture in the US surrounding guns—a culture which tragically seems to value accessibility to guns over human life."

Veronica Lurvey, Co-Founder of North Shore Action and Town of North Hempstead Councilmember

---

"This book is a riveting account of the pain suffered due to gun violence, and the journey to hope, healing and peace."

Elder Audrey Lewis, Friendship Baptist Church, Roslyn, New York

---

"Gun Violence isn't a Black or white issue, it isn't a Democrat or Republican issue, it isn't a young or old issue, and it isn't a me versus you issue. Gun violence is a human issue. Irresponsible people have used guns to destroy our families, our schools, our entertainment venues, our faith-

based institutions, our streets, and our homes. As a responsible gun owner, I beg our law makers to be agents of change, to take a look at how guns get into irresponsible hands and address the crisis we face."

Shanequa Levin, Award Winning Social Justice Leader, Founder/CEO Women's Diversity Network

"Fight for the things that you care about, but do it in a way that will lead others to join you."

— RUTH BADER GINSBURG

CONTENTS

Introduction	xvii
1. The Macabre Dominance of the Pro-Gun Minority *Martha Rosenberg, Chicago, Illinois*	1
2. Vicarious Survivors and Our Role in Advocating for Collective Healing *Sabrina Spotorno, Port Jefferson, New York*	9
3. How I Survived Gun Violence *Mary Hennings, St. Louis, Missouri*	17
4. Steven *Ron and Norma Molen, Salt Lake City, Utah*	33
5. Fighting Against All Odds *Tom Vanden Berk, Chicago, Illinois*	41
6. The Long Island Railroad Massacre *Joyce Gorycki, Mineola, New York*	53
7. The Death of My Brother *Leah Gunn Barrett, Scotland*	61
8. Do Not Stand Idly By (Leviticus 19:16) *Rabbi Joel Mosbacher, New York*	69
9. Bewilderment *Elliot Fineman, Chicago, Illinois*	73
10. That Fateful Day *Rose Pagano, Providence, Rhode Island*	83
11. The Indelible Day *Alvin Glazier, St. Louis, Missouri*	99
12. My "Story," or How I Came to be Passionate About Gun Violence *Christine Ilewski Huelsmann, St. Louis, Missouri*	111
13. Sandy and Lonnie Phillips *On the road in an RV*	125
14. Guns and a Heart of Flesh *Rabbi Shaul Marshall Praver, Newtown, Connecticut*	135

15. Our Hearts Are Broken *Risa Zwerling Wrighton, St. Louis, Missouri*	143
16. A Short Story of Becca *Marlene Eldemire, Maineville, Ohio*	153
17. Reflection *Trenelle Gabay, Brooklyn, New York*	159
18. Never Again *Paul Guttenberg, Commack, New York*	171
Afterword	185
Acknowledgments	195
About the Author	197

"It is not in the stars to hold our destiny, but in ourselves."
William Shakespeare, from "Julius Caesar"

INTRODUCTION

The purpose of this book is to demonstrate that gun violence has claimed the lives of many innocent people.

At any given moment, the easy accessibility of guns results in devastating losses of innocent lives. There are the victims and the victimized, otherwise known as survivors.

Contained within these pages is a compilation of stories written by eighteen people located in various states throughout our country - some who were personally affected by gun violence, others who were not. The others included are professionals whose lives were indirectly affected who voiced their unequivocal cry to eliminate the easy accessibility of guns that resulted in senseless deaths.

I am deeply grateful to these people, survivors or not - brave souls, who agreed to contribute to this book project.

These include people from many walks of life and different states, whose only common connection is the loss of life due to the gun and gun violence.

Those who were personally affected may be considered victims, but they refuse to be victimized. Rather, they consider themselves to be survivors. The victims were those who were lost, loved ones, whose lives were suddenly and senselessly cut short.

These are their stories. They are all true stories written about and by people from various parts of our country whose lives were impacted and changed forever due to the accessibility of guns.

My first book, *The Unthinkable: Life, Loss and a Mother's Mission to Ban Illegal Guns*, was written about my daughter, a victim of gun violence. Ironically, I was a gun safety advocate even before her death.

The media covers the massacres. Those are numbers. Not even names.

However, each of those numbers had a face, a family, friends.

The Unthinkable focused on the life of one person and the devastating effects that an unconscionable act had on our family and friends, to create a personal attachment.

The following stories are indicative of human resilience, turning tragedies into advocacy, activism, the preservation of life and justice.

Their actions to rid our country of the easy accessibility of guns demonstrated their own human strengths and emphasized the beauty of the lives of their loved ones, if not the lives of a future generation.

As a member of the Jewish community, my goal for this book project was to gather eighteen submissions. The number eighteen in Hebrew means "Chai," or "to life," or "for life." In other words, to affirm life.

However, I do not mean to only reflect my Jewishness. These stories are about affirming life, no matter the race, creed, color or religion. They are about turning tragedies into activism, advocacy, the preservation of life and justice.

The Reverend Martin Luther King said, "Our lives begin to end the day we become silent about things that matter."

Life matters.

L.S.

1

THE MACABRE DOMINANCE OF THE PRO-GUN MINORITY

MARTHA ROSENBERG, CHICAGO, ILLINOIS

"All mankind is divided into three classes, those that are immoveable, those that are moveable and those that move."
~Benjamin Franklin

My name is Martha Rosenberg and I am an anti-gun violence advocate.

Many people became aware of gun violence after massacres like Columbine, Virginia Tech and the many mass shootings that have occurred since 2007. However, because I was living in New Orleans in the late seventies, I became aware of the epidemic much earlier. In fact, New Orleans was way ahead of the rest of the nation when it came to gun violence.

I remember walking down Canal Street, the major retail street that borders downtown New Orleans and the French Quarter in the middle of the day. Some children—maybe 8-10 years old—were walking in front of me and other children of the same age were walking behind me. One boy had been fighting with another one over a hat. As the group in front of me was walking away, a boy behind me yelled something to re-instigate the fight, perhaps calling the boy in front "a pussy." Suddenly the boy in front of me who had been walking away, turned around, produced a gun, put it into the other boy's stomach and fired.

Since I was between the two groups, I naturally got out of the way when I saw the gun—quickly moving to the side where the store fronts were. After the shooting, my boyfriend ran after the shooter—who had already dropped the weapon — and captured him. He did it because the police were on strike at the time. "The gun was bigger than he was," remarked my boyfriend. The victim died.

Around the same period of time, a tourist on Royal Street—a block from where we lived in New Orleans' French Quarter—was held up at gunpoint for his money and fatally shot in the head. I did not hear it but a neighbor of ours witnessed the entire bloody sequence. He said the gunman was shaking so much, it was not even clear that he intended to shoot. Soon after that, a guard at a Quarter hotel only about two blocks away was also shot in the head and died. Many times after that, tourists who had simply ventured a few blocks away from the lighted "nightlife" area of New Orleans' Quarter become gun violence victims according to the news.

Though I knew nothing about gun laws at the time and did not question how the shooters got their guns, I did begin to believe that almost anyone in New Orleans was carrying a gun and that you could be shot at any moment for no apparent reason at all. The gun violence was a big reason that I moved away from New Orleans.

Fifteen years after I left New Orleans, the gun violence was still raging. In 2004, the rock musician Ray Davies, front man of the music group the Kinks, was approached by armed robbers while walking with his girlfriend on Burgundy, a street that borders the French Quarter. Many people were in town for the Sugar

Bowl match between Louisiana State University and Oklahoma at the Superdome.

Davies said an armed mugger appeared and fired one round into the ground to show that the gun was loaded, then asking for all his money. When Davies refused, the mugger grabbed Davies' girlfriend and put the gun to her body, again demanding money. Davies complied. After ascertaining that the girl was okay, Davies pursued the mugger who turned and opened fire, hitting him with a bullet that went straight through his leg.

According to the New Orleans Times-Picayune newspaper, Davies' alleged assailant Kawan Johnson was never brought to trial but his cousin, Jerome Berra who drove the getaway car was charged twice. The case was dismissed twice because Davies failed to appear in court to testify (though he said he was notified of the trial only days before he was asked to appear and couldn't make the trip from London).

I have always been an animal lover and this also increased my awareness of gun violence. When Vice President Dick Cheney's hunting party killed 417 pen-raised, defenseless pheasants at a Pennsylvania canned hunting club in 2003— Cheney killing 70 himself—I became aware of the gratuitous canned and sport hunting that the gun lobby supports and thrives on. I continue to be appalled that "sportsmen" kill animals whose meat they don't need simply because they enjoy shooting animals.

Around the same time as Cheney's hunting spree, the NRA began an aggressive push for workers to have the right to bring their guns to work even as mass shootings, including those at workplaces, were skyrocketing. The NRA began casting gun owners as "victims" whose "rights" were oppressed by gun safety laws. The irony of wanting to carry lethal weapons everywhere but somehow being "victims" was not lost on me.

In 2004/5 three shootings captivated the nation: a six-year veteran of the California National Guard shot and killed six on a Wisconsin hunting trip; a parishioner at the Living Church of God shot and killed seven during a church service, also in Wisconsin and a young man on the Red Lake Minnesota reservation shot and killed 7.

Still, the gun lobby was able to pass the Protection of Lawful Commerce in Arms Act in 2005 which protects firearms manufacturers and dealers from being held liable when crimes have been committed with their products. This is when I became an activist.

As I studied the gun laws, I was shocked at how successful the gun lobby has been in securing the "gun rights" of its extremists at the price of public health. How, for example, did the Tiahrt Amendment that prohibits the National Tracing Center of the Bureau of Alcohol, Tobacco, Firearms and Explosives (ATF) from releasing information from its firearms trace database to anyone other than a law enforcement agency or prosecutor in connection with a criminal investigation—actually helping criminals—become law? Or the law requiring ATF to destroy background check data within 24 hours? Was the nation, including myself, asleep at the wheel when these laws were passed?

Psychologically I began viewing gun extremists as King Babies: bullies who want to carry their guns everywhere yet want to consider themselves victims at the same time. Afraid to go where normal people, including the old, children and 80 pound women go without their guns, they are like "fear biters" in the dog world.

Further evidence of the bully/fear personality of gun extremists was revealed in 2012 when the Journal News published the names and addresses of handgun permit holders in two New York counties. The self-proclaimed law-abiding gun owners sent packets of white powder to Journal News employees and issued death threats including threats against employees' children. Worse, the gun bullies won and the permit holder information was censored.

There were several ironies in the Journal News story. First, as with the Tiahrt Amendment and the Protection of Lawful Commerce in Arms Act, gun extremists were requesting help from the same "jack booted government thugs" who they say want to take their guns, in this case to keep their identities anonymous. Second, commensurate with their fear personalities, gun owners said the published public data about their gun owning would "put them in danger" despite their mantra that only guns keep someone safe.

As a feminist I am also keenly aware of how women in the US are killed almost every day by armed and angry husbands and intimate partners, despite orders of protection. Often these bullies kill the women when they try to leave; often they kill family pets first. Clearly these unbalanced people should not have guns. But that's not how pro-gunners see it.

Pro-gun Justice Clarence Thomas articulated the gun lobby position well in 2016 when arguing that domestic abusers should not be denied gun rights. "Give me another area where a misdemeanor violation suspends a constitutional right," he asked, later suggesting that the particular domestic abusers in this case shouldn't lose their ability to carry guns because they've never actually "use[d] a weapon against a family member." He should have added "yet."

The barely disguised racism of the NRA is also no secret. Musician Ted Nugent, one of its board members, has worn a Confederate flag shirt when he performs. After Hurricane Katrina, a new NRA brochure (never published) was leaked that showed white people defending themselves with guns on the roofs of their homes from African Americans.

There are several industries in the US that are widely seen as putting the public at risk for financial reasons such as tobacco, chemical, gas and oil companies and even Big Pharma, in light of the opioid epidemic. But the macabre dominance of the pro-gun minority, stems not just from money but a mental disorder characterized by aggression and bullying, control, paranoia/fear and often sexism and racism.

Martha Rosenberg is a nationally recognized public health reporter who covers food, drug and gun safety. She contributes to British Medical Journal (BMJ), Consumer Reports, Public Citizen, the Center for Health Journalism at USC Annenberg, the Nieman Foundation for Journalism at Harvard University and other top outlets. She also contributes chapters to medical textbooks.

Rosenberg's FDA expose, "Born with a Junk Food Deficiency," was named as part of "One Book One Chicago" in 2016 and praised by Public Library of Science, Library Journal, Vice and the London Times. Rosenberg won a Northern Illinois Newspaper Association award in 2018 for work in the Evanston RoundTable.

Rosenberg has appeared on CSPAN, National Public Radio and lectured at the medical school and university levels.

Martha Rosenberg

2

VICARIOUS SURVIVORS AND OUR ROLE IN ADVOCATING FOR COLLECTIVE HEALING

SABRINA SPOTORNO, PORT JEFFERSON, NEW YORK

> *"The sacred rights of mankind are not to be rummaged for among old parchments or musty records. They are written as with sunbeam in the whole volume of human nature by the hand of divinity itself and can never be erased or obscured by mortal power."*
> ~ Alexander Hamilton

The day I met Lois at the Youth Over Guns Walk on the Brooklyn Bridge I immediately felt her compassionate energy. I also sensed a wisdom that comes from personal suffering long before she shared her story with me as a survivor of gun violence. After that meeting a thought grew, one that I have had for a long time but only increases in frequency with each day that effective gun safety legislation does not get passed: do we listen to our survivors? We sympathize with their pain and share in the experience of their trauma to these various forms of gun violence, but do we really appreciate the strength they have in getting up and living in a nation that repeatedly sends messages of minimizing what they have been through?

As a clinical social worker I am called to bear witness to survivors' pain, strength, and ideally, their healing. I am also called to advocate for when social problems need to be handled on a larger scale. I am trained in the ecological perspective, one that focuses intervention in the context of the transactional relationships between an individual and the multiple systems they interact with. This framework allows focus on the immediate crisis or social problem and long term preventative interventions to reduce it; it is not just the how to get out of a metaphorical hole approach, but how to fill in the hole so that it is not a hazard. We can all agree gun violence is a multi-dimensional social problem. After each tragedy we all ask- what could have been done? What sort of mental health issues led the shooter to get to that ultimate form of violence? This is where I am weary of how much the blanket term of "mental health issues" becomes just that, a blanket term to simplify a very complex situation. The heavy stigma this creates does not just potentially deter people that could benefit from any level of therapy from utilizing it, but often leads to villainizing those with severe mental health diagnoses as "high risk violence initiators." According to the American Psychiatric Association, only 1% of individuals diagnosed with a mental health disorder can be classified as a threat to self or others. Any gun related killings are largely due to suicides according to this same study, furthering the case for proper gun regulation enforcement to reduce access to means during a critical need for such. From my own clinical experience across the boroughs and Long Island, I can attest to many survivors and family members of victims that met the criteria for PTSD, struggling with both the stigma of utilizing mental health services and being invalidated of the pain they face.

Another aspect of all this is the importance of research to align with effective measures. Ethically we are responsible for funding programs that align with facts related to risk factors and interventions; this holds true for any public health issue. Gun violence fatalities are almost equivalent to motor vehicle fatalities -33,636 and 33,804 per year, respectively- yet the federal government allocates $240 million per year to traffic safety research and practically nothing to gun violence research due to the Dickey Amendment, which prevents such acquisition of knowledge. How will we develop policies that support families that have suffered a loss of a loved one to gun violence as well as policies for survivors of gun violence to best treat their PTSD symptoms? And how will we fund proper research so that we don't use blanket explanations?

We hear survivors and victims not just in the literal sense but more importantly through our actions on the individual, local, and national levels- through the cultural norms we live by. Survivors continue to be retriggered by the uncertainty of another attack because our validation of their trauma is not as swift as it needs to be. If it was, marginalized communities would receive proper funding to ensure health and safety, gun safety legislation would be comprehensive, and platforms for continued growth would be standard institutions. I will never forget struggling to aid an individual with finding a way to relocate or having their landlord change the door on their apartment, since it still had the bullet holes from the home invasion two years prior. The system to help was in place, but the backlog and the lack of funding for these resources is what we need to change.

On several occasions, my children and adolescent clients have spoken so indifferently about all the escape routes they have for every single classroom they are in during the school day. I have to use supervision to cope with these encounters as I often see their faces and hear their voices whenever I hear of another school shooting or death by gun violence; something that I know clinicians and advocates can relate to when they recognize that those we lose are OUR children. Language is so important here: it is not someone else's child that is lost to gun violence, it is OUR future leader, OUR future creator, OUR future, period.

"There can be no keener revelation of a society's soul than in the way in which it treats its children." Nelson Mandela's poignant words have also been on my mind for quite some time now and I cannot think of a more succinct way to drive home the message for our nation. Our children deserve so much more. Students should not have to anticipate an act of gun violence on school grounds, our younger generation should not have to live in fear the rest of their lives, and our future generations should not be in the same chronic trauma of never knowing a time where school shootings or any other forms of gun violence were not standard parts of our culture. A well known trauma study in the field, called the Adverse Childhood Experiences Study (ACES), indicates alarming changes in individuals' health based on the amount of toxic stress experienced in childhood. People that scored 4 or more on the test were two times more likely to develop Hepatitis or COPD, four times more likely to develop depression, twelve times more at risk to die from suicide. In other words, we are not just living in a world where survivors are not heard but developing a generation of survivors that will have long term health consequences if we do not make the conscious effort to provide interdisciplinary care and prevention.

My activism journey took full swing during the time I worked on a degree to specialize in substance use treatment. Student leaders created the platform at the school for gun safety reform advocacy, a movement that originated from marginalized groups for some time that are only now starting to get their voices heard in the mainstream discussion of this public health issue. I met many inspirational individuals from different walks of life, different reasons for being involved, and yet one common mission to see a safer community today and beyond.

From these amazing souls, my fellow student leaders were able to be involved in several marches, events, and even attended the NYS DNC, where we heard Joe Biden speak, and his words have resonated in terms of just how incredible our nation is when we remember the values we believe in. He described how no other nation can involve the most resilient people from all over the world, not just to celebrate each other's differences, but to use them collectively to create increased quality of life. We need to work to maintain that, complacency is giving in to those wishing to oppress these brilliant minds and justify that oppression as status quo. He also summed up America in one word: possibilities. We all have a right to those possibilities and with everyone's involvement we can ensure that our future generations can reach a healthier environment than our own. My hope is that everyone can continue to listen through action and share their stories, just as those who have been threatened or oppressed in the past have done, so we can continue to learn from injustice and evolve into a more compassionate society.

Sabrina Spotorno (she/her) is a Licensed Clinical Social Worker (LCSW) and Credentialed Alcoholism and Substance Abuse Counselor (CASAC), in New York, New Jersey, and Oregon. Graduating summa cum laude from Adelphi University, she had a generalist education with training in several modalities, including Trauma-Focused Cognitive Behavior Therapy, Compassion Focused Therapy, Systemic Family Therapy, Dialectical Behavioral Therapy and Narrative Therapy. A strong believer in integrative approaches she continues learning about new modalities, with a recent study in Liberation Based Healing and Polyvagal Theory.

Having worked in several outpatient substance use and mental health clinics, she has joined the virtual platform Monument as a clinical operations manager to provide accessible services to individuals looking to change their relationship with alcohol. She sees a strong connection between clinical work and advocacy work to ensure destigmatizing and decolonizing of mental health and substance use treatment. Her passion is to empower clients to increase their sense of acceptance, value of self care, and realization of their inner wisdom to live and speak their truths. You can find Sabrina at joinmonument.com where she conducts individual sessions as well as moderating support groups on the platform.

Sabrina Spotorno

3

HOW I SURVIVED GUN VIOLENCE

MARY HENNINGS, ST. LOUIS, MISSOURI

"In spite of everything that was done to me and my race, in spite of the adversity and the bitter moments, again we rise."
~Maya Angelou

If life is an illusion, in the end, I believe it is a very good one. This is the life that I know as the reality we are living and what I've been through. Gun violence has played a major part in my life. But with it all, I have maintained my faith in humanity and God.

I remember that Wednesday morning so clearly. The date, September 27, 1989 at 3 a.m., I received a telephone call from my mother....saying, "He's dead, Mary. He's dead."

Quickly, I jumped out of my bed, hung up the phone and looked for something to throw on to get over to my mother's house.

I ran to wake up my two children, Michael, who was 11-years-old and Kim, 14-years-old. I told them to hurry and get dressed.

They were confused and still too sleepy to really understand what I was saying. Then, I said, "Just grab your shoes. You can put them on in the car."

I got the keys to the car and the three of us rushed out of the house. We lived in the Blumeyer Housing Development in St. Louis at the time.

As I got into the car, all I was doing was asking God not to let it be.

Michael wasn't saying a word, but Kim kept asking what was wrong. I couldn't tell them that their brother might be dead. I just kept saying out loud, "Please God, don't let it be." I took Dr. Martin Luther King Drive straight over to Belt Avenue. It seemed as if it was taking forever to get to my mother's house.

When we finally pulled up to my mother's house, the door was wide open but I couldn't believe no one was there. I felt like it was all a dream. I felt empty inside. Was this really happening to me? As I was getting back into my car, my mother pulled up. She told me to follow her to Barnes Hospital.

The words kept spilling out of her. She told me that Alvin, my oldest son had been shot and the ambulance had taken him to the hospital. This wasn't the first time he was shot...it was his second.

The first time he was shot in his hand was by one of his so-called "friends" while he was in the alley on Belt Avenue. He was 15 years old.

Later, I questioned Alvin as to what had happened. He told me that he shot himself. I took his word for it but I didn't really believe him. I had strongly warned him about being around guns. I guess that's hard for some boys...cars, guns and girls...the things most boys like get them in a lot of trouble sometimes.

It was another long ride to Barnes Hospital. I needed to know what was going on with my son. We finally made it to Barnes Hospital.

I started questioning the nurses. I wanted to know whether my son, Alvin Hennings, was a patient and whether he was alright. They weren't telling me anything.

But the nurse kept asking me about my insurance for the hospital and who was going to pay the bill. The nurse and I kept going round and round. She kept asking me about my insurance information and I kept asking if they were going to let me see my son if he was in fact, a patient. Then, I asked her why would I give her my insurance information when I wasn't even being told if he was a patient and if I hadn't seen him in the first place.

Finally, they confirmed that my son was at the hospital.

They led me to the room to identify him. I knew it was him when I walked through the door and saw his feet and how they set apart like he was "slew-footed." My eyes followed his body all the way to his head where I saw blood running from his eye like red tear drops, dripping and falling to the floor. I touched his body and he was sweaty, wet, like he had really been hot.

I will never forget the touch of his warm body. It felt like he had just passed. I felt like he was trying to hold on; waiting for me to get there. Sometimes our children are defiant towards us. Why didn't he listen to me? That's what I was asking myself. If only he had listened to what I had to say about guns he would've been alive...and now he's gone, never to be seen again.

I was lost...I ran into a girl I know and she told me that she thought I was on drugs... "No," I said, "I just lost my son." I was confused and didn't care about how I looked.

Now, 32 years later, no one has ever been charged in his murder. I still pray to this day that the coward who took Alvin's life is caught and charged.

It has been rumored lately, that the "friend" who was in the alley with Alvin when he was 15 years old was the one who killed him. I see that guy often in the neighborhood and still wonder if the rumors are true.

He has never told me he was sorry for my loss. The two boys grew up together and spent time with each other practically every day.

To make matters worse, my sister noticed the casket was open. She asked the funeral director why it was open. I had two assumptions. Either the person that killed my son hid the murder weapon or his father came to view the body because he did not attend the funeral He had only learned about his son's death on the news.

The funeral director confirmed that someone had opened the casket but that it but it would be closed. That was hard for me to hear. I have never stopped thinking about it.

Life goes on and I have always focused my attention on my other two children. I had to catch myself because I frequently felt myself drifting away. I kept thinking what I might have done wrong with Alvin so that I could do better with Kim and Michael. Being a single mother, and not having the children's father around was hard.

I remember when he "flipped out" on drugs. He sawed off a rifle and attempted to kill me because I wanted to have a break from him. It was like the day he said he was going to California because he didn't want us to get tired of each other and needed to get away.

I never felt he ever really loved me. He never showed me any affection. He was always with his friends. I was only 13 years old when we got married, and think to this day that I never should have gotten married in the first place.

The day he attempted to kill me was a close call. I was on the phone talking to my sister. He actually shot the gun through the window while the police were outside. I managed to get out of the house and don't think he knew I was gone. I could see him through the mirror on the closet door with a gun in his hand. I played it off. I went towards the front door to get my keys, but he had taken them out of the door lock. He claimed he didn't know where my keys were when I asked him about them. I knew he was lying because they were the only ones we had in the house. So, I walked towards the back of the house, went down to the basement and crawled to the other side of the flat where my neighbors lived and went out their basement door. I escaped.

I never called the police because he threatened that if I did he would kill me. It wasn't until later that I learned my mother called the police. I scurried around the building and saw the place crawling with police.

Later, I discovered that he had pulled the phone from the wall. I was sure he would have killed me if I had not gotten away because he shot the rifle and a bullet went through the window across the street from where we lived. That is when I ended the marriage.

The kids and I regrouped trying to get it together, eliminating all of the in-between stuff that goes on when life happens.

I dealt with the fact that my son, Alvin was gone and there was nothing I could do about it. I did the best that I could to keep the family together. I was grateful that I had Kim and Michael. I had lost one son, I dreaded losing another. Alvin's murder caused a lot of anguish and confusion within me. I even wondered whether I was too possessive with my children.

Kim graduated from high school, got married but later divorced. She got a job and is still working to this day. However, she was also affected by gun violence. Kim's ex-husband was shot three different times. He survived, disabled, but alive.

But Michael was growing up, turning rebellious and was influenced by peer pressure. I always tried to keep him out of trouble and juvenile detention.

Although Michael never married, he ended up having six beautiful children, five girls (I am raising Mikayla, my oldest grandchild) and one son. That son was born on May 8th, which was Alvin's, birthday. The birth of that little boy gave me some hope that things were finally getting better. I believed that God had not forgotten about me and he was putting a little sunshine back in my life. My family was starting to grow and that made me happy. Michael seemed to be staying out of trouble. I didn't want to lose him like I lost his brother. I would constantly talk to him about life's challenges trying to save his life...asking him what he thought he might be in the years ahead of him.

On October 25, 2013, I was going to visit Michael. Suddenly, as I was about to step onto his porch, I felt a heavy impact on my inner thigh and collapsed. The pain is hard to explain, but it was an immediate sharp pain. I wondered what the hell it was and what happened to my leg? Then I heard gun shots and loudly shouted that I had been hit.

I looked around to see if anyone else was hurt. I saw my brother, Anthony, Michael's God-brother, laying down on the sidewalk near Michael's car. His friend, Verdie, told me to get into the house. He said that he had noticed a little blue car on the street that looked suspicious. Me, being me, told him not to be so paranoid.

But then, I saw another person running across the corner lot. Then, I saw a guy shooting from a black Charger with an Uzi which had an extended clip attached to it. He was wearing a black hoodie but I saw his face and head. I couldn't see the car's driver nor could I see if anyone was sitting in the back seat. My eyes were focused on the shooter and I wondered when was he was going to stop shooting or run out of bullets. Meanwhile, I feared what had happened to me. I kept asking God all kinds of questions and to please not let me die.

I tried to pull myself up to hide behind the brick wall on the porch, but no luck. The pain was so great that I just couldn't move at all. It felt like the house itself was holding me down. I kept calling Michael's name but he never heard me. He was in his house never realizing what was happening on the outside.

After a while I saw a car speed down Belt Avenue and turn right. Then I heard them go up the alley. The last I heard before they fled the scene were two more shots.

Anthony ran over to me and stooped down. He started hugging me as the blood gushed from my thigh like water from a drinking fountain. Anthony saw there was a lot of blood, stood up, took off his shirt and tied it around my leg as a tourniquet to control and stop the blood from coming out. I then asked him to get my son after he pulled me to the top of the porch.

I will never forget the look on Michael's face when he came to his front door. He thought I was dead until I opened my mouth and told him to get me off the porch.

It took the police a very long time to get to the crime scene. But when the first responder came, I asked him what kind of bullet I was shot with. He told me a 9mm and asked if anyone shot back. I said no one had. The only shells that they found were from the gun used to shoot me.

I was dismayed while in the hospital that not one detective came to see if I was alright. They never questioned me as to what happened and what I might have seen.

To me, the police didn't care. I called the detective in charge of the case to find out who shot me. He told me that Michael knew and to ask him. He then hung up on me.

I questioned Michael. He said he didn't know. Besides, he was in the bathroom at the time.

I was thankful to God for keeping me alive, but sad, and still experience a lot of pain resulting in difficulty in walking. I thought, I never did anything bad to anyone to deserve being shot, and now I have to rely on others to help me get around.

Just when I thought things couldn't get any worse, five months later on April 2, 2014, Michael was murdered right in front of his house. It happened during a severe thunderstorm, with loud, consistent thunder, lightning and jack ball/quarter size hail coming down. My stepfather called and said "to brace myself." I asked, "Brace myself? For what?" He told me there was a shooting in front of Michael's house. Michael and a woman were in a car and sitting motionless.

I rushed out as fast as I could. But it took me longer than it normally would due to the gunshot wound. I finally arrived, which was about 15 or 20 minutes later. I saw an ambulance just pulling out and my son and the woman were still in the car. There were so many policeman and detectives milling around the scene of the car. The car was sitting there, bloody and ugly. I started walking towards the passenger side of the car, when a detective stopped me at the yellow crime scene tape.

It was a massacre. The woman and my son were both killed with an AR-15. That was the second time Michael was shot. The first time, while he was being robbed and was only shot in the foot. This time, he died.

The police finally charged someone, seeking the death penalty for those two murders, my son and the woman he was with.

The detectives told me that they didn't want me to see the deformities caused by the assault rifle. I was permitted to read the autopsy report but couldn't finish reading it because I was so overcome with uncontrollable tears. Later, I learned that the girl was decapitated. This is an example of just how powerful the AR-15 is.

Kim called me one day to tell me that a butterfly had flown into her car. She was reminded that I had once told her about what it meant. I told her that I had read that it was her loved one letting her know that they were alright on the other side. I don't know if it's true or not but it's a good thought to help me get through my children's demise or for anyone going through the loss of a loved one.

It made me think of how that dove during Michael's burial flew under the canopy trying to set on Kim's shoulder. It scared and startled her but didn't settle. It flew back outside of the crowd.

I Googled information about purgatory three nights in a row after Mike's passing. The thought was waking me up. An article popped up on the afterlife and what may happen on the other side. I don't know. But it's good to have thoughts that may help me feel better, knowing that my sons are never coming back to me in the flesh.

I read an article that mentioned something about premonitions and remember having a conversation with Michael just before he died. The article said something about the deceased that made them feel the transition of death was coming and if they said a certain something to just one person they wanted them to help catch a killer. I did just that ... started searching.

The grief that I go through about my two sons is really hurting me. Reading that article and wondering if it may be true put me on the road to help find Michael's killer and help stop the violence. I have seen more murders reported in the news since Michael's death than I have seen in all my days, which was corroborated by a St. Louis police chief.

I look back on that meaningful conversation. Michael shared many thoughts with me that day that I will never forget. It might have confirmed the premonition of his imminent death. He told me about how if he never lived another day that he was proud of his accomplishments, helped many people, took care of his children and had fun doing and seeing things.

But he then sat down on his couch and said he was tired. He was murdered the next day.

I have a strong belief in God. Taking lives that God created and devastating families, some dying from broken hearts. What is it all for? I would like to know.

Knowing that God is real gives me the strength to carry on. It's through his Grace that I am surviving these tragedies . Losing a child is devastating. But to murder? It's the worst feeling anyone can ever encounter. How can anyone hate so much as to take another person's life?

So God is my strength to carry on. We have to go through trials and tribulations. Maybe this is the sacrifice I have to go through in order to get to God. He knew how much I loved all my children and knows that they loved me if no one else in the world did. They were all I had. They were my life. That's what I lived for. I did the best I could to raise them to be decent and respectable people. I tried my best to keep them alive.

My life has been turned upside down due to gun violence. I began to lose all hope because of the easy accessibility of guns, and gunmen are literally getting away with murder…everyday.

I needed to do something to help myself, as well as others, to survive and to honor my sons' memories.

One day I went to a march against gun violence and met STL Mothers In Charge. It was an event scheduled to take place at the Demetrius Johnson Center in St. Louis. Like me, they were all mothers who had been victims of gun violence. They were a breath of new hope.

They seem to have given me the motivation that I needed to help make a difference in attempts to STOP THE VIOLENCE. They have been a strong support system for me. Without it, I think I would be lost. If I keep losing people that I love and care for, I don't think my heart could continue to be so strong.

Gun violence puts a permanent void in people's lives. We all need to speak up in order to stop the gun violence and other crimes against each other.

I feel the pain of other parents, relatives and friends who have to endure this never-ending grief.

I have lived in neighborhoods where guns are accessible, people walk around with them, lives like mine have been turned upside down and gunmen are literally getting away with murder....everyday.

We must come together to end the violence in our city and abroad. To show with the help of our community that we can achieve this positive goal.

We all share a common bond to reach a common goal - by stopping this senseless violence and other forms of chaos.

Since my sons' deaths I go out advocating against gun violence to save other lives.

I tell people about how gun violence has affected my life in many ways - losing two sons, I myself being shot and never having the shooter or killers apprehended.

My life was stolen, a part of me was taken and can never be replaced.

WAKE UP AND SPEAK UP, HELP SAVE OUR EXISTING CHILDREN. SHOW THEM THAT THIS IS NOT THE NORMAL WAY TO LIVE. VIOLENCE IS NOT LOVE, AND ANGER IS NOT THE ANSWER.

I hope my story can reach the hearts of other people and that I am truly understood.

This is a troubled world. Together with my faith in STL Mothers In Charge and my faith in God I can help make a difference to stop the violence.

> Mary Hennings was born in Memphis, Tennessee on January 4, 1956. She was the first-born of 7 children. Her mother was a single mother and moved to Saint Louis, Missouri when Mary was a year old. Mary settled down and had three children: Alvin, Kimberly, and Michael. She went on to pursue her aspirations of being a barber and got both her cosmetology and barbering licenses. Her quick-wittedness, advocacy, and zeal have allowed her to become part of many community organizations and activities such as being a Sunday school teacher, advocate for stopping gun violence, and helping local politicians run their campaigns. In 1989, Alvin, her first son was murdered, and later in 2014, Michael —her last child— was murdered, too. Though the lives of her two boys were senselessly stripped away from them, she was blessed to have had six grandchildren, all of which are descendants of Michael.

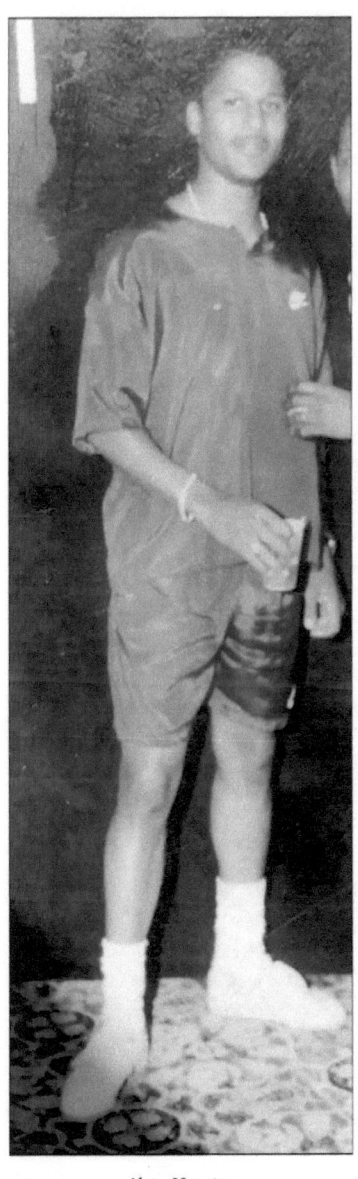

Michael Hennings

Alvin Hennings

Mary Hennings

HOW I SURVIVED GUN VIOLENCE | 31

Mikayla Hennings' school art project, drawn in April, 2015 with her grandmother's help depicting his last words of Michael, her father before he was murdered.

4

STEVEN

RON AND NORMA MOLEN, SALT LAKE CITY, UTAH

"A man as a general rule owes very little to what he is born with, a man is what he makes of himself"
~ Alexander Graham Bell

Our son Steven was murdered on April 23, 1992 on the fourteenth floor of the graduate dormitory at Indiana University.

Steven was dating a graduate student who was being stalked by a German ex-boyfriend who was currently a doctoral candidate at Stanford University. She had met the German during her study abroad. The relationship quickly terminated, but the German never accepted it. Many threatening phone calls followed the entire year, but the distance between Palo Alto, California and Bloomington, Indiana made her feel safe.

The evening the tragic event took place, Steven was studying in his dormitory room when he heard a gunshot and a scream. He ran down the hall, tackled the German stalker, whose 22 pistol had misfired. Steve quickly pinned him to the floor. The girl stood at the door of her room, screaming. A floor monitor arrived, grabbed the pistol from the floor, then insisted Steve release the stalker. Steve let him go and immediately the stalker reached in his backpack and pulled out a Glock pistol. He shot Steven, the girl, and then himself. Paramedics rushed Steven to the hospital while the other two were pronounced dead at the site.

A doctor called us that evening telling us that Steven had been shot. He was on life support and that we should come as fast as we could. I called our daughters, Jill and Lee, and our son, Mark. They insisted on joining us, but we suggested they wait until we arrived at the hospital and found out what the situation was.

We arrived in Bloomington at 10 the following morning and found Steven hooked up to machines that breathed for him and kept his heart active. Clearly, Steven's condition was dire. We tried but failed to reach the children by phone. An hour later the three of them walked into the hospital. They had disobeyed our instructions, but we were extremely grateful.

Following five days of tests, the doctors determined that Steven was brain dead and there was no way for his body to function without the machines. We had to make the terrible choice of taking him off mechanical life support. That night his young, healthy heart was flown to a patient waiting in Indianapolis.

A memorial service was held for Steven in Salt Lake City where friends and family spoke. Several days later we scattered his ashes on a prominent site in his favorite canyon. Governor Evan Bayh, who later became Senator Bayh of Indiana, posthumously gave Steven a state award for bravery for rushing to the defense of the girl.

We now had to confront the reality of a lost son and brother whom we would never see again. Of course, we had each other for support but each of us had to work through the acceptance on our own. Norma attended grief therapy sessions and I wrote Steven a daily letter for several years.

Steve had a special relationship with each of us. He loved the long talks he had with Jill, who had just given birth to her first baby.

His favorite subject was the purpose of life, and at age sixteen he decided there was no God and insisted we all join him in his atheism. Jill listened patiently and kept her faith.

He counseled Lee that her boyfriend, who did not read and who was addicted to television sports, was not good enough for her. Lee eventually married a voracious reader who never watched a football game in his life.

Steve was convinced his older brother, Mark, was a genius, probably because he was gifted in math that Steve found so difficult. But they liked to discuss their commitment to science and reason over a glass of beer at the pub.

And for his parents, he had a special calling to remove us from the Mormon religion he knew we could not possibly believe in.

We also had a lot of external support. Randall Lake, a prominent artist, told us he had an unfinished portrait of Steven we had no idea existed. It is a spectacular portrait that catches the essence of the intellectual young man, the iconoclast, the disciple of James Joyce. Randall insisted that we accept it and we were overwhelmed by his generosity.

Steven was a gifted writer and excelled in literature as a writer and as a critic. He majored in English Literature in college. At the age of 23, his first short story was included in an anthology called "Flash Fiction" with famous authors, such as John Updike, Raymond Carver and Joyce Carol Oates.

Steven was fascinated with the Old Testament as literature and his professor submitted Steven's complex interpretation of the

Bible story of Jacob wrestling with the angel to a Jewish rabbinical quarterly where it was published. Steven died before he saw his work in print.

So we have many icons of Steven's short but full life, but the most comforting are the personal memories of the happy child, the adolescent appalled by the inequities in the world and the tender young man who loved teaching English to second grade children in Taiwan.

During our anger stage we started an organization now called "The Gun Violence Prevention Center of Utah" that evolved into the current Gun Violence Prevention Center. I wish that I could report some success with the Utah Legislature, but in almost the 30 years have passed, promiscuous gun laws have increased. 120,000 Utahns carry concealed weapons, and guns are now legal in churches, schools and on college campuses.

The Unitarians, Catholics, Episcopalians, Presbyterians and Methodists have stood with us on gun control issues but the LDS Church and Evangelicals have remained silent on this gigantic moral issue. Fearing a loss in tithing was given as an excuse for the Mormon Church.

We shall continue to campaign because we, like many parents who have lost a child, feel an obligation to demand a change. We had a very bright and promising child who would still be alive had he been born in any other advanced nation where guns are tightly regulated and death from firearms is extremely rare. And the German murderer had to come to this country where the means to kill was as readily available as wine in France.

Norma spoke on the steps of the Lincoln Memorial at a huge national rally for gun control. It was a heady experience that accomplished nothing. Since Steven's death, over 1.5 million Americans have been killed by firearms and well over a million were wounded.

We found ourselves among many families who had lost a child or had one permanently maimed. No matter how the death occurred, the final result was the same. A child was lost. I do not know that I have any great advice to give except that we can promise hope. Time heals. And after many years, it will not be the first thing you think about when you wake up in the morning, or the last thing on your mind when you retire at night.

The one positive change I can report is that, at last, after almost 30 years, families like ours find ourselves as part of a majority who demand intelligent, well-crafted regulations. We must work to replace those politicians who refuse to address gun violence and replace them with legislators with common decency and common sense and with a heart and soul.

Thank you for the opportunity of sharing our story.

Ron Molen grew up just outside Chicago in Northern Indiana. As a child he had the good fortune of many visits to the Chicago Art Institute. Later a high school art teacher told him and a close friend that both had a future in art. Ron's friend became a well known artist and sculptor while Ron chose architecture. Following a mission in Switzerland and Austria he attended the University of Utah and graduated in 1958. He attended a sketching class from Leconte Stewart and water color classes from George Dibble, Harold Olsen, and Roger Bailey. His profession required sketching and watercolor renderings, but he and his wife only became serious painters in the last fifteen years. They have built the last three houses with an art studio where they spend several hours every day and where crits of each others' work flows freely. Together they studied with Bonnie Posselli and David

Evans and twice spent a week with Ed Maryon and Doug Snow at Carmel.

Ron works in water color, acrylic, and oil and has exhibited in statewide shows as well as local galleries. He likes a great variety of subject matter, but Utah landscapes are his favorite. He tries to include something man-made that fits gracefully into a natural scene to prove human development doesn't have to violate nature. He writes daily and has published nineteen novels, a number of essays, and 2 books on architecture as well as Letters to the Editor in the Salt Lake Tribune exclusively on gun violence. Following their son's death, he and his wife Norma started an organization called The Gun Violence Prevention Center of Utah that is more active now than it has ever been. Since Norma's death, Ron has written and produced three videos with a separate web page called Utah Representative Democracy.

Norma Lowe Molen was born April 17, 1930 in Grace, Idaho, a small town where she was related to half the inhabitants and where her parents Mary Anne and Moroni Lowe were pillars in the community. With five older brothers her parents were thrilled to at last have a girl. She attended school in Grace and Montpelier, the University of Utah, the LDS Business College, and finally received a BFA from Westminster College.

She married Ron Molen in 1955 and they had two sons, Mark and Steven, a daughter Jill, then Lee joined the family. Norma's mother also lived with the family until her death in 1972. Norma was a splendid daughter, wife and mother, and she also excelled as an artist. Her oils, water colors, and pastels won many awards and were exhibited in local galleries. She loved to travel to foreign countries with her husband and their trips often included her children or friends. She enjoyed book clubs, dinner groups and, after her son Steven's murder, helped found an organization now called The Gun Violence

Prevention Center of Utah. The results of her numerous activities were many lifelong friends.

Norma suffered the last decade of her life from a failed spine operation, but never gave up. She was swimming with her husband just a week before her stroke.

Her daughters and husband were present around the clock during her time in the hospital and her few days at home. She was surrounded by family members on September 28, 2017 when the peaceful end came. She will be greatly missed.

Randall Lakes painting of Steven Molen

Steven, Norma and Ron

Painting by Ron Molen

5

FIGHTING AGAINST ALL ODDS

TOM VANDEN BERK, CHICAGO, ILLINOIS

"The key to success is action, and the essential in action is perseverance."
~ Sun Yat Sen

My name is Tom Vanden Berk. Gun violence has had a major impact on my life.

In the early 1970s, when the war in Vietnam was raging, I chose to be a conscientious objector rather than serve in an unjust war. The alternative service I was assigned was to be a child welfare worker in Chicago's Lawrence Hall, an agency caring for abused and neglected youths and their families in Chicago, Illinois. I remained at Lawrence Hall for 16 years and, while there, married and had two children, Chenel, my daughter born in 1972, and Tommy, born in 1976.

While raising my children in Evanston, a progressive suburb of Chicago where I hoped they would be exposed to diversity, I continued my work in child welfare, serving as executive director of Chicago's Uhlich Children's Home.

Though Uhlich provided residential treatment for foster children and youths in the care of the state, gun violence was not on my radar screen. Certainly I realized that the kids we worked with were neglected and did not come from caring, loving families but I thought such kids from difficult communities were most vulnerable to gun violence.

In 1992, my daughter had enrolled at Georgetown University in Washington D.C. and my son was a sophomore at Evanston Township High School, a large, academically acclaimed public school with 3,393 students.

Tommy was a "struggling" honors student. He had great potential, but I had to crack down on him so he would give more attention to his grades. He loved skate boarding and was a budding and popular disc jockey.

The night I lost Tommy in 1992 he had asked if he could go to a party in a nearby neighborhood where he had a chance to perform as a disc jockey. I drove him and his closest friend, Chris, there and, after ascertaining it looked safe, dropped him off at 8:30, planning to pick him up at 11.

Around 10:30 Tommy called me and said he had not had a chance to spin music yet and could he stay until midnight? I said, "No, I told you I would pick you up at 11:30," but Tommy wanted to negotiate. "I've improved my grades a lot recently, Dad," he said, so we agreed on midnight.

When I arrived at midnight I could not get near the party location, police cars and fire engines were everywhere and the street was blocked off. The police stopped me and I said I was looking for my son. Suddenly Chris appeared and he said, "I think Tommy got shot." A nearby police officer confirmed that a young man had been shot and said he had been taken to the nearby Children's Memorial Hospital.

Somehow I drove to the hospital and pulled into the ER where security intercepted me. I told them I thought that my son had been shot and they said that was not possible because the victim was African-American. They did not realize that Tommy was biracial.

What followed is an experience too many parents have endured and will continue to endure. I was put in a solitary room and a chaplain came in to tell me Tommy was gone. I became physically sick. After a while, I was allowed to be alone with my son, never to see him alive again. He looked strangely at peace to me.

I called a neighbor to tell my wife what had happened so she would not be alone when she received the news. After I got home, my wife and I got tickets to fly to Georgetown that night so we could tell Chenel about her brother in person. She flew home with us the next day.

In the following days, my family and I were able to piece together what had happened. After the party, some well-known gang bangers had invaded the building and simply started shooting. Since the party had been upstairs, Tommy had hurried down the stairs to escape but was shot in the alley by one of the gang bangers. He had died instantly.

Fairly quickly, detectives came to our house to meet with my wife and me. "We've arrested six individuals aged 14 thru 21 in the shooting," they told us. "We should let you know since this will be in the newspapers tomorrow."

My first emotion was that I wanted to kill the young men who had taken Tommy's life. I had no sympathy for them -- no thought of forgiveness. I was also unable, emotionally, to be in the same room with the killers or attend the trial. It turned out that I only had to be in the courtroom twice, once for opening identifications and once for a victim impact statement that I gave.

The man who killed Tommy was found guilty and sentenced to 50 years in prison. At least one of the accomplices walked free because he was under age. To this day, I still don't know how the gun was acquired, if it was recovered, or how many times Tommy was shot. For a while I did not care if I lived or died.

AFTERMATH:

The board of directors I worked for was extremely supportive of me in the months and years ahead, giving me the kind of help few bereaved parents receive. But since I already was working with disadvantaged kids, I became haunted by the question of how could these kids get access to guns? I began to learn about gun violence.

I contacted James Garbarino, an author and professor at Loyola University in Chicago, who studied the causes and impact of violence in children and was able to tell him about my trauma. Dr. Garbarino has consulted to the National Committee to Prevent Child Abuse, the National Black Child Development Institute, the U.S. Advisory Board on Child Abuse and Neglect and other groups.

Dr. Garbarino put me in touch with knowledgeable gun violence experts in the government, at foundations, and in anti-gun violence groups that existed or were forming. Some were modeling themselves with state chapters like the successful Mothers Against Drunk Driving, or MADD. I began attending conferences about gun violence, meeting academic figures who were seeking to establish gun violence as a public health problem and reaching out to well-known authors. Significantly, I studied the gun lobby and especially the NRA to understand how they have established the pernicious and deadly gun culture that exists in the United States.

I soon realized that with my professional and personal experience, I could be the voice for gun victims and began doing public speaking and then lobbying. In Chicago, I worked with former Mayor Richard Daley for better gun laws pitting us against the strong Illinois gun lobby. At the federal level I was able, with other committed anti-gun violence activists, to achieve a sunset of the law that made assault weapons legal -- called the "assault weapons ban" by the press.

TODAY:

After my experiences, I became the driving force behind the creation of the Gun Violence Prevention Political Action Committee (G-PAC), a non-partisan political action committee which since 2013 has worked to counter the political influence of the gun industry and its lobby efforts in Springfield, Illinois, the seat of the state's government. G-PAC raises the resources necessary to protect and elect public officials with the courage to stand up to the gun lobby. G-PAC provides campaign support to legislators committed to keeping guns out of the hands of criminals, gang members, domestic abusers and the dangerously mentally ill.

The loss of my son has helped me work to repeal dangerous gun laws and enact gun laws that will save lives. But, as every parent like me knows, gun violence leaves a permanent scar and sense of emptiness. For example, my marriage was not able to withstand the loss, and we divorced. I also sometimes suffer from self-recriminatory thoughts like, "Should I have refused to let Tommy remain at the party?" or "Should I have raised him in a place that had less crime?"

However, the loss of my son has also given me undisguised anger at public officials who refuse to change gun laws and made me resolve to beat the gun lobby at its own game. The local and federal lawmakers who allow dangerous gun laws to stand or refuse to pass gun safety laws are a direct result of terrorist-style pressure from the gun lobby. "You will regret voting for this gun safety law," say these violent, pro-gun lobbyists.

Fortunately, the groups I work with have found the same tactics work on our side. "If you oppose this gun safety law which will save lives, your constituents will soon know how you voted," we are able to say to lawmakers and have had fantastic results. "If you do not support gun safety laws, you will pay with your legislative seat and your livelihood."

From my long work with troubled youths and government organizations, it is very clear to me that "awareness" and "education" will not stop gun violence. Forcing lawmakers to pass gun safety laws will.

"Unlike the multitudes who bemoan the violence and do nothing to help, Tom Vanden Berk has spent his life helping."

-- *Chicago Tribune columnist Mary Schmich, June 9, 2016*

Widely regarded as a passionate and outspoken leader in youth welfare and violence prevention, Thomas Vanden Berk has devoted 49 years to improving the lives of abused, neglected and dependent children in the Chicago area.

As CEO of UCAN (Uhlich Children's Home Advantage Network) from 1987 to 2016, and now as UCAN CEO Emeritus, Vanden Berk has been a hands-on change agent in strategic planning, fundraising and nonprofit management, and led the organization from its role as a shelter for 50 boys and girls on the brink of closing to the forefront of child welfare agencies in Chicago. In early July 2016, he transitioned into the role of CEO Emeritus at UCAN where he continues to focus on social justice issues, particularly the disproportionate homicide rate among youths of color, and fundraising for UCAN.

An avid advocate of UCAN's vision that "youth who have suffered trauma can become our future leaders," Vanden Berk has been a recognized supporter for implementing a culture and practice that fosters positive youth development. Today, UCAN serves more than 11,000 youth and families, and is a leader in trauma-informed treatment, violence prevention, youth development and diversity and inclusion. UCAN's clinical approach to healing is united, culturally relevant and consistent.

Vanden Berk suffered the loss of his 15-year-old son to gun violence in 1992 but has turned anguish into determination, becoming instrumental in informing and educating a long list of child welfare organizations on the importance of strategies to combat gun-related deaths, disability and suffering.

He founded HELP for Survivors, a victim self-help support group for parents and others who have lost children or loved ones to the gun violence epidemic. He is a founding member of The Bell Campaign (eventually known as the Million Mom March), and has served as a board member of the nationally respected Brady Campaign, whose mission is to create a safer America that will lead to a dramatic reduction in gun deaths and injuries.

Over the years, Vanden Berk has been profiled in the media for his passionate support of reasonable gun restrictions. Regarding Chicago's ongoing and still mostly unsuccessful campaign against gun violence, in a June 2016 profile of Vanden Berk, Pulitzer Prize-winning *Chicago Tribune* columnist Mary Schmich wrote: "Has anything gotten better? All I know for sure is that without the work of people like Vanden Berk, things would be a whole lot worse." Titled "Chicago's persistent violence and a father's fight for change," Schmich's moving column called Vanden Berk "an ardent local voice for gun restrictions — not a ban, but tight registration laws, pressure on owners and dealers."

Tom Vanden Berk is the subject of, and source for, dozens of news media features and stories that chronicle the gun violence in the Chicagoland area and nationally, as well as the impact of trauma in youths' lives to support and motivate those who are most directly affected by exposure to trauma.

Tommy Vanden Berk

Tom and Neli Vanden Berk

FIGHTING AGAINST ALL ODDS | 51

Tom Vanden Berk

AT EVERY AVAILABLE OPPORTUNITY, Vanden Berk cites sobering statistics that spell out how each year in Illinois an average of 1,000 people are killed by gun violence and countless others are seriously injured; most are children. The devastation imposed by this epidemic on communities and families is unimaginable. He eloquently repeats how polls show that a majority of gun owners and non-gun owners alike favor sensible gun safety measures to save lives.

A board member of the Youth network Council who frequently speaks on gun violence and has testified before the U/S. Senate Judiciary Subcommittee, Vanden Berk has actively worked with Chicago Mayor Rahm Emanuel on the implementation of sensible gun laws in Chicago. He servers on the governor's Illinois Anti-Violence Commission and is an advisory board member of the NIU Center for Child Welfare & Education; and advisory board member of the Dominican University School of Social Work; and birch member of the national Runaway Switchboard. The Council for health and Human Services Ministries named him the 1998 Executive of the Year.

6

THE LONG ISLAND RAILROAD MASSACRE

JOYCE GORYCKI, MINEOLA, NEW YORK

"When you reach the end of your rope, tie a knot and hang on."
~ *Abraham Lincoln*

I believe that I was born with a sixth sense. Unfortunately, it is a foreboding one.

The date was December 7, 1993. Shortly after the Thanksgiving holiday, I had a premonition that something dreadful was going to happen to my husband, James. We had been happily married for fifteen years and were blessed to have given birth to our daughter, Karen, who was ten years old that year.

Jim was born in Merrick. I was born in Malverne. When we married we lived in Mineola, Long Island and I have remained as a resident there.

Nationally, December 7th was referred to by President Franklin Delano Roosevelt as the "day of infamy," after the bombing at Pearl Harbor. Personally, it was a "day of infamy" for me, too.

On that morning, Jim and I were getting ready to go to work. Jim was in the hallway of our apartment, gathering all his belongings together before leaving.

Like any other typical morning, he would travel to the Long Island Railroad's Merillon Avenue station. He became friends with a father, Dennis McCarthy and his son, Kevin. The three men's friendship deepened over the years as they traveled to work together. Jim always told me how he "got a kick" out of the McCarthy's warm father/son relationship.

They shared stories of their lives and family. Dennis was married to a nurse whose name was Carolyn.

As Jim was leaving, I asked, "Did you take your lunch?" He immediately held it up and said, "Got it, and see you tonight."

There was a strange feeling I had and do not know whether it was my foreboding sixth sense or whether God was telling me that would be the last time I would see my husband.

When I came home from work that night I heard my neighbors in the apartment house talking about a shooting at the Long Island Railroad's Merillon Avenue station.

Then Karen told me the same news.

I immediately turned on the television and tuned into the Channel 12 Long Island news station. The newscasters were giving full blown reports about the shooting.

Further uneasiness erupted in my stomach.

Friends and family knew that Jim traveled to and from the Merillon Avenue station and kept calling me to see if he was home or even heard from him.

My brother, also named Jim, called me. Emphatically, he said, "Stay home with Karen," and volunteered to go to the site.

I waited for hours, hoping against hope that my husband was not involved.

Around 10PM there was a knock at the door.

I just knew it was the police.

I opened the door looked straight at the two policemen and said to them, "My husband was killed."

"Yes," they quickly answered. I collapsed to the floor.

I managed to collect myself, and shakily walked to the sink to get a glass of water.

My brother Jim and his son-in-law John arrived, having learned the same news returning from the Merillon Avenue station.

The police told me that someone had to go to the morgue to identify my husband's body. As I recall, the expressions on the policemen's faces were filled with compassion, and they desperately tried to console me as best they could.

I was so grateful that Jim and John said they would go to the morgue for me.

That night we drove to North Merrick to tell my mother-in-law the tragic news. It was a blessing to have had my mother-in-law's close neighbor come to her house for support during this critical time.

I do not know how I gathered the strength, but I made a myriad of phone calls to family members and friends to tell them the devastating news and to make plans for the wake and the funeral.

I couldn't believe the enormous amount of people who came to Jim's wake and funeral. Tom Gulotta, the Nassau County Executive even closed the parkway exits for the funeral procession until the cars arrived at the cemetery.

Bob, my other brother, flew in from Arizona to be with us.

I received many letters and cards from total strangers because the "Long Island Railroad Massacre" was in the national news for a long time afterwards. I even received invitations from the media asking me to do radio and television interviews. It was all overwhelming.

Let me tell you there are a lot of good people in this country. Six of those good people senselessly died that day and nineteen were injured during that massacre because one madman got hold of a gun. Among them, was Jim, my beloved husband, and Dennis McCarthy. Kevin miraculously survived but now uses a walker.

Shortly after the massacre, Karen and I moved to Scottsdale to be near my brother Bob. I thought the change would be good for us to remove ourselves from the place where we were faced with devastating memories.

We remained in Scottsdale for 10 months but missed our surroundings and returned to my Mineola roots.

Upon our return, I kept receiving requests for interviews to appear on news programs on gun violence because the enormity of the massacre had not subsided.

I have always been rather shy when it came to public speaking. But that shyness was dismantled. This was about the death of my own husband. There was no question about it. I had to face this tragedy, head-on, to honor James' memory and for my own sense of well-being.

Those interview requests were to my advantage and I welcomed all of the media invitations. I let myself "roll" with it.

I wanted to publicize the facts about gun violence and that I was living proof about the tragic effects it has on ordinary citizens like me.

I ended up participating in press conferences on gun violence, giving radio, television and cable speeches and interviews in front of thousands of people. I even surprised myself that I could actually do this.

It was only after the massacre that Carolyn and I bonded.

We became staunch advocates against gun violence and gun safety and each of us fought in our own way. But the message was the same. We did not want another tragic death to happen to another family.

Carolyn became the much admired Congresswoman whose candidacy was focused on gun safety. I am proud to acknowledge that my advocacy has been acknowledged with many awards in addition to becoming the Chairperson for the Long Island State Chapter of the non-profit organization New Yorkers Against Gun Violence and participating in the Million Mom March in Washington.

Gun violence needs to stop. Bills need to pass. We need a national law for background checks, regulating purchases of guns and also the types of guns being purchased.

More than twenty-five years have passed since the incident. For the first ten years, Carolyn and I would conduct a memorial service on each anniversary, leaving wreaths for our husbands at the Merillon Avenue train station.

After 9/11 we both were so totally overwhelmed that we could not continue this tradition. But we will never forget.

I will continue to speak out for gun safety. I will never give up.

My sixth sense tells me several things. My husband is looking down, seeing all of this. Yet, my predictions about the future are foreboding but hopeful.

Joyce Gorycki lost her husband, James of fifteen years in the "LIRR MASSACRE" on December 7, 1993.

She became a committed activist, first joining the non-profit organization, New Yorkers Against Gun Violence, a board member for 25 years, and the former chair of the Long Island chapter. Joyce has spoken publicly on the issue of gun violence at many press conferences, radio, television and cable broadcasts. Her activism has been written about in countless newspaper and magazine articles as well as books.

She was featured in director Charlie Minn's documentary "LONG ISLAND RAILROAD MASSACRE" which was released in November, 2013. Joyce's activism has earned her many honors. They include:

-1997: "Long Island United Way's Strength & Courage Award" as the keynote speaker for their annual fundraising event.

-2000: inducted into the "Women's Role of Honor" from the Town of North Hempstead.

-2004: "Trailblazer of the Year Award" from the 9th Legislative District of the Nassau County Legislature.

-2004: recipient of the Newsday and Adelphi University's "Everyday Hero."

-2007: received the "Outstanding Activist Award" from New Yorkers Against Gun Violence.

-2008: "Women of Distinction Award" from the 17th Assembly District.

-2010: "Women of Distinction Award" from the 7th Senate District.

-2014: Pax Christi "Peace Award" along with Congresswoman Carolyn McCarthy.

-2019: On June 4th, received a "Proclamation for being a committed activist of NYAGV" with others of the organization from the County Executive of Nassau County.

Jim and Joyce Gorycki

James (Jim) Gorycki

7

THE DEATH OF MY BROTHER

LEAH GUNN BARRETT, SCOTLAND

"Action is eloquence."
~William Shakespeare, from "Coriolanus"

My life changed forever the evening of March 3, 1997. It was an ordinary late winter day in London. I had just returned home from work and was starting dinner for my kids and in-laws, who were visiting us from Boston, when the phone rang. It was my brother, Mark, who shouted down the line that Greg, our older brother, had been shot that morning in Tulsa, Oklahoma. He was in the hospital and was brain dead. Could I please come as soon as possible? It's hard to recall what I said next but I remember feeling stunned and confused and panicked all at once. I think I screamed.

It wasn't clear what had happened. Greg had gone to work that morning and when his wife tried to reach him, he didn't answer his phone. She found him slumped up against the back door of his business. There was some blood but it wasn't apparent where it had come from. She thought maybe he had fallen and hit his head. She called 911 and the fire department came, cleaned up the scene and took him to the hospital. When he was x-rayed it became clear that he had been shot. The .38 caliber bullet had entered through his forehead and lodged in his brain. He was on life support. It became apparent then that cleaning up the crime scene was forensically disastrous.

I booked the first flight out of London the next morning and flew in a mental fog to Tulsa where my father picked me up from the airport. We drove straight to the hospital where I found my family and Greg's two teenaged children waiting in the corridor outside his room. Brooke, 15, and Bryant, 13, looked so lost and confused and I felt my heart breaking. I hugged them both before entering the room. Jeanine, his wife of 17 years, was in a black leather easy chair by his bedside, where she had slept the previous night. Periodically, she would gently wipe blood that oozed from the bullet wound in his forehead. She told me that they had waited for me to arrive so I could say goodbye. I remember taking my brother's large left hand with its gold wedding band and squeezing it. It was rough and warm. I think I whispered that I was so sorry and that I loved him. Jeanine kept talking to him, saying how much she loved him and that she had given him the best years of her life. Her mother, Rosemary, in a wheelchair because she had undergone heart surgery the week before, was with her daughter. The nurse came into the room and asked if we were ready. We nodded and she then switched off the ventilator. Then we waited and watched as the color drained from his face. Greg was forty years old.

Greg was my older brother. I was the second child and only girl to be followed by three more brothers. I always sensed that it was hard on Greg being the oldest. He could have used more of my mother's attention and because he was the oldest, more was expected of him. He was a wonderful swimmer and had a long, lean body that sliced through the water when he swam breaststroke. Of the five of us, he and I would most easily tan and would compete on who would be browner at the end of the summer. I remember how his light brown hair would bleach blonde, accentuating his green eyes. Shortly after Greg's murder, I dreamed that he came to me on a bicycle, all tanned and golden. He seemed so real. I asked if he was all right. He smiled and told me that he was in a good place and that I shouldn't worry. I cling to that dream.

Greg was a rebel and gave my parents a hard time when he became a teen. He moved out of the house during his senior year in high school, which really upset my mother. However, when years later he reconnected with his first love, Jeanine, and proposed marriage to her, I knew he would be all right. They married the summer after my college graduation and settled in Tulsa. She was the perfect partner for my brother and it was clear they loved each other very much. Two beautiful children followed and Jeanine and his children were the center of his world.

I remember when, as children, Greg and I would ride in the car with my paternal grandfather in Tulsa, Oklahoma as he ran errands, took us to his favorite cafeteria, Furr's, or to the amusement park with the Zingo roller coaster. He would complain that the "niggers" were ruining the town and was upset that black families were moving into his neighborhood, negatively impacting property values. But he was a wonderful grandfather, who read us stories, showed us Halley's comet from his back yard, took us to Indian Pow-Wows, taught us how to graft pecan trees, grew watermelons that we ate on his back patio, made jam from his strawberries, baked chocolate brownies covered in powdered sugar, and was always there for us.

Our grandfather died in 1976. Many years later I learned about the 1921 Tulsa race massacre. My grandfather was born in 1900 so he would have been 21 years old. In just 16 hours in the black middle class neighborhood of Greenwood, over 800 people were injured badly enough to be admitted to the hospital and around 10,000 were left homeless. Thirty-five city blocks with 1,250 homes were destroyed by fire and many more suffered millions of dollars worth of property damage. The Red Cross estimated that 300 black citizens were killed, making this the worst massacre in US history. I wish I could have asked my grandfather what he remembered about these massacres. What was he doing at the time? Did he think these people deserved this level of death and destruction? How did the massacres poison race relations in the future—how did it impact my grandfather's views, how did his views shape my own father?

My father, a local doctor in Kansas, employed two smart competent black women, as an office manager and secretary. For over 20 years, my mother employed a lovely woman to help her clean house one day a week. Her name was Reola Wilson. She was illiterate and had 17 children. As a child, she picked cotton in Georgia with her sharecropper parents. My mother was the one to tell her about birth control and took her to the doctor to get fitted with an IUD, so she wouldn't have to have any more children. Miss Reola, as we called her, lived in the poor part of town. My mother told the story that once when she took Miss Reola home, Greg, who was six at the time, exclaimed, "But her children are black!" as her kids streamed out the house to greet her. He had not made the connection that she too, was black. To him, she was Miss Reola who called him "Greggy-boy" and gave him frequent hugs. I could always tell that Greg was her favorite.

After Greg's murder, my family and I moved back to the US and I became involved in the gun control movement, first in Maryland and then New York. I didn't know of any other way to honor my brother than to fight against the epidemic of gun violence that killed him.

It didn't take long for me to make the connection between our nation's ugly history of slavery and racism and its equally ugly gun culture. I learned that the Second Amendment was in large part included in the Bill of Rights because southern colonies wanted to ensure they could put down slave rebellions with firearms. The data shows that blacks are far more likely to be victims of gun violence than whites and we all know that the police are more trigger happy when confronting a black person, even one who is legally armed. The so-called gun rights activists, who are regularly whipped into a frenzy by the largest terrorist organization on US soil, the NRA, are merely the tools of a craven gun industry desperate to increase its profits. The NRA knows that fear sells. And fear of the other people (who are different from the older white male demographic buying guns) is the surest way to fuel gun sales. The main reason Americans buy guns today is for self-defense, at a time when crime is at historic lows.

Greg was murdered that March day over twenty-five years ago by a black teen in Tulsa, Oklahoma. He was a petty criminal and drug user from a broken family. Because he had a gun, he used it to kill Greg, who was my brother, Jeanine's husband and Brooke and Bryant's father. This young man is in prison and will remain so for the rest of his life. I wonder how his life's trajectory was influenced not only by the Tulsa massacre but the countless other instances of injustice and discrimination that have poisoned our nation. Would Greg's murder have been preventable had slavery not have happened? I don't know. But one thing I do know with blazing clarity is if that young man had not been able to get his hands on a gun, Greg would be alive today. My years working to prevent gun violence have taught me that if you get rid of the guns, you will get rid of the gun violence. But because those who supposedly represent us are unwilling or unable to tackle the real problem—the obscene proliferation of guns—Americans will continue to die and be maimed at horrific levels.

I am writing this from Edinburgh, Scotland, where I have chosen to live. Gun violence is rare in Scotland and the rest of Europe. In April 1996 in the small Scottish town of Dunblane, sixteen 5-year-olds and their teacher were killed by a disturbed man armed with a handgun. Within eighteen months, the UK Parliament responded by enacting a law banning the civilian ownership of handguns. Contrast that with the pathetic inaction from a puerile Congress following Columbine, Virginia Tech, Fort Hood, Aurora, Oak Creek, Sandy Hook, Charleston, Orlando and too many others to name.

I have many friends in the US who continue to bravely soldier on, fighting against the corporate gun lobby and its political stooges. Their goal is simply to save lives. As much as my heart is with them in their struggle, I do not believe this uniquely American nightmare will ever end.

Leah Gunn Barrett is the former Executive Director of New Yorkers Against Gun Violence and CeaseFire Maryland. She served as a Dean at Columbia University's School of International & Public Affairs and held senior management positions in London with The Economist Group, Data Resources (DRI) Europe and Tetra Pak UK. She has a B.A. in Economics and Russian from Carleton College, a Master's in International Affairs from Columbia University, and a Master's in Teaching from Johns Hopkins University. She lives in Edinburgh, Scotland.

THE DEATH OF MY BROTHER

Greg Gunn

Leah Gunn Barrett

8

DO NOT STAND IDLY BY
(LEVITICUS 19:16)

RABBI JOEL MOSBACHER, NEW YORK

"Mankind must remember that peace is not God's gift to his creatures, peace is a gift to ourselves."
~ Elie Wiesel

Gun violence was an issue that I cared about as a Jewish kid growing up in suburbia. It was one of many issues I cared about in a meaningful way, even though it wasn't from a personal place.

That all changed in January, 1999, when my father Lester, one day short of his 53rd birthday, one month short of celebrating the first birthday of his first grandchild, was gunned down at his place of business. My whole life, and the life of my mother and my whole family, was changed forever.

We endured so much loss; in that moment, we joined a terrible club that no one wants to be a member of—the families and victims of gun violence—that grows by 30,000 each year.

As I began to emerge from the horror of my grief, I began slowly to realize just how pervasive this problem is, and how numb we Americans have become to this scourge. Surely, if 30,000 Americans were dying in a war each year, we wouldn't simply stand idly by while our neighbors bleed.

And yet, it seemed to me, most Americans seem to accept the plague of gun violence as one of the prices of being American. Because if we didn't accept that price, we would have done something about it by now.

It was only some 11 years later that I found something to do with my pain and my anger and frustration. It was only 11 years later that I began to tell my story publicly. It was only 11 years later that I told my younger son, named after Lester, how his grandfather had died.

It was only when I felt like there was something productive I could do with my story that I found the courage to tell my story. It was only when I found a way to work together with people across lines of race and faith and class to act powerfully to reduce gun violence that I began to tell my story, to share my anger, to stop standing idly by myself.

The "Do Not Stand Idly By" campaign, created by the Metro Industrial Areas Foundation, seeks to use the massive purchasing power of our police and military, who collectively buy 40% of the guns in this country each year, to press gun manufacturers directly to reduce gun trafficking and innovate in gun safety technology.

Under the Obama administration, over 100 mayors, police chiefs, sheriffs, and governors have committed to using their buying power to demand accountability from the gun companies who have produced and sold the 300 million guns that already exist in this country. The work of broadening and deepening the use of public purchasing power to press manufacturers to help reduce gun violence has continued into successive administrations.

Those companies can dramatically reduce gun trafficking by holding their worst dealers, those 1% of dealers who are responsible for the sale of 60% of guns that turn up at crime scenes, accountable for their sales practices. And they can create safer, personalized guns that can only be fired by authorized users, so that children might not shoot themselves or playmates with a gun belonging to a parent, so that people in an emotional state might not so easily harm themselves or others with a gun they know is in the house, so that shiploads of stolen guns would be useless to those who stole them, and so that police officers couldn't be shot with their own service weapon.

I struggled to make sense of the murder. Words of consolation from some well-meaning friends were "that it would make me a better rabbi" due to this tragedy.

My response was, "Well, I'd rather be a terrible rabbi and have my father back."

Nothing will bring my father back. Nothing will bring him back to his beloved bride, my mother. Nothing will bring him back to his grandchildren.

But if telling my story can prevent even one other family from having to go through what my family did, I'll keep telling my story.

We can change this terrible trend in our society. I think we're ready, finally, belatedly, to begin.

Rabbi Joel Mosbacher serves as the Senior Rabbi of Temple Shaaray Tefila on the Upper East Side of New York. Rabbi Mosbacher's tireless efforts to combat gun violence first began in 2012 partnering with the Metro Industrial Areas Foundation, the nation's oldest and largest network of community organizing.

He now serves as a national co-chair of the "Do Not Stand Idly By" campaign to reduce gun violence donotstandidlyby.org. Clergy, citizens, police, elected officials, and institutional investors have joined together to press gun manufacturers to innovate in gun safety technology, and to hold their dealers to the highest distribution standards.

Rabbi Joel Mosbacher and his dad Lester Mosbacher at the Rabbi's wedding

9

BEWILDERMENT

ELLIOT FINEMAN, CHICAGO, ILLINOIS

"Pray like it all depends on God and then when you are done, go work like it all depends on you."
~ Martin Luther King

When the news came, beside the paralyzing shock to my entire being - physical, emotional, spiritual — a cloud of bewilderment covered it all. And to this day—some 10 years after my son was murdered—I remain bewildered. How could it be? How could this be?

There is no getting over this unimaginable and unnatural loss, nor would one ever want to. It being ever present is a measure of one's love and one's eternal connection to their missing child. It is a bond that can never be broken.

On the afternoon of December 30, 2006 I was talking to my son Michael, who lived in San Diego. He had just returned from an RV camping trip to Mount Zion National Park with his family. He wanted to send me color pictures from the trip and, as I did not have a color printer at the time, he told me to go to CVS and get the phone numbers he needed to send and set them up for printing.

I did and we were to talk the next day about the logistics. But we would never speak again.

On the morning of December 31, 2006 a Chicago police woman came to my door to tell me that my son had been murdered the night before in San Diego while having dinner with his wife and another couple.

We would find out later that his killer was a paranoid schizophrenic who had been in mental institutions twice, yet was legally able to buy the gun he used to kill my son.

When I was able to function, which took considerable time, I closed my practice—I was a strategic marketing advisor to Fortune 500 companies and decided to bring that skill set to the gun issue. I also formed the National Gun Victims Action Council (NGVAC) to focus on strategic solutions to the gun violence epidemic.

There are things that are fixed in my mind's eye from that morning; my oldest grandson saying that his dad would never see him when he was 10 years old, and Nancy, my life partner, standing by the window gazing out in utter confusion. This did not fit with her understanding of how God worked and was present in our lives and reflected in each of us. Telling my daughter to drive down from Evanston where she lived to my place in Chicago.

She kept asking me if Michael was dead and I kept saying just drive down, just drive down. Later she would tell me she knew, as she had gone online to check the story. I remember talking to the San Diego police officer that had been on the scene after the shooting. I kept asking for an explanation of what happened and how, but he had very little information other than to tell me that my son's body was in police custody, as this was a murder investigation.

I made three trips to California subsequent to Michael's murder—one the very next day, one for his memorial service about three weeks later, one for his military honors funeral 30 days after that. Because this was an open murder investigation, we could not bury Michael until the police gave permission.

How did it happen? Michael and his wife and another couple who I knew had gone to an upscale dessert restaurant after having gone to the theater. While they were eating, a derelict person who did not really belong in the restaurant, suddenly hovered over their table mumbling incoherently. Michael asked if he could help him and after more mumbling Michael explained how the restaurant worked, that you gave your order at the front, they gave you a number, you put it on the table that you sat at and they brought your order to you.

The killer said, "You go find a table." (I know this because the husband of the other couple—who also was shot but survived—told me what had happened.) Michael, who was a combat medic with special forces and a psychological-ops expert, immediately said to the waiter, "Call 911—these things escalate quickly." But they did not call 911. Instead, they escorted the intruder outside and 11 minutes later he returned with his gun that had been in his van and put four bullets in my son's head and the remaining two bullets in the shoulder and chest of the other husband.

Everyone in the restaurant panicked, hid either under tables or fled and my son's killer walked away into the night.

I began to talk to the San Diego DA every week afterward, hoping that my son's killer would be captured and taken off the streets. I did not want revenge nor did I have an instinct to want to forgive or understand and I feel that way to this day. I just wanted him prevented from ever doing this again to anyone. But there was no progress.

Finally, we were able to get the story on *America's Most Wanted* and within 24 hours the killer's truck had been identified and he was apprehended without incident.

I never went to see Michael's body. I never wanted to remember my son in what I imagined was the condition he was in. I wanted to (and do) remember him for the indestructible force he was and for the warmth everyone—even strangers—felt when he entered a room.

As a combat medic he had been in the most dangerous places in the world and yet he lost his life in a restaurant in San Diego. He also had his own business and was an award-winning designer focused on remodeling, space and lighting design. He had the twin natures of both an artist and a soldier but if he had none of that it would not have mattered—what did mean all to me was that he was my son.

He had solved the problem no one had before—how to finish a construction project on time and on budget. He was writing a book (I was helping him with it) and had taped the first part of an infomercial to advertise the construction project solution. I still have the tape but have never been able to look at it. Perhaps I will someday along with his three children (my three grandchildren) but none of us have had the composure to look at what was so suddenly and permanently—taken away. Michael's incredible, loving mother had passed away—a victim of cancer—when he was 17. Nancy, who had subsequently come into my life and was my life partner on every level, lost her life to lung cancer in 2012. Thinking of watching Michael's tape without her makes it all the more difficult.

How did I continue, how did I go forward or to use Michael's term "soldier on?" I was in a cloud, bewildered and had no life force or life energy. People sent me material to read (especially my daughter) but they were just words and had little impact. There was one book—"When the Bough Breaks" written by two professors who had lost their son to a brain aneurysm.

They had studied families that had lost a child at least five years ago to any cause; illness, violence or an accident. The mother described the comfort she got when she went to a supermarket and saw someone who looked like her son and followed them around all the time they were there.

I too have seen people who walk like my son, are built like my son and for a time I followed them as well.

All the people I've met who have lost a loved one—and especially a child—want to do only one thing with their lives and that's to prevent others from having to go through what they have gone through. That is where I am and will stay for the duration.

Two friends said meaningful words at the time, but they were just that—words. I heard them but did not respond, nor was I consciously moved by them. Yet I remember them, so there had to have been some impact somewhere inside of me.

One said that we are biological constructs and that when our system is disjointed and displaced it ultimately must return to equilibrium. That what I did now and felt did not matter, all the life energy that was gone would ultimately return no matter what I did.

The other said that the cosmos is always sending energy and we are always receiving it whether we are aware of it or not—that ultimately the energy I did not have, the life force, the interest, the capacity to participate would all return irrespective of what I did.

I heard their words but did not respond or focus on them. Maybe they were right and life force would return, but it made no difference to me whether they were right or whether my life force would return.

I don't know how I was able to continue or how I found a way to continue. I do know I did virtually nothing to move forward and generate life energy. I did see a grief counselor for several months. While they had no formula or keys to "unlock me" I mainly talked and they mainly listened—I always felt a bit better after our visits. I don't know why, I just did.

I could not give anyone going through the same experience today a process, a blue print, a method. My life energy did come back—not suddenly, not noticeably—but it came back.

I remember a moment of unbearable guilt when three months later, I was reading something and laughed. I was horrified. I caught myself and could not understand how I could possibly laugh when my son was dead.

About a year later I went out of town to a two-day seminar on a topic that I had had specific interest in for many years. As is the practice at these seminars, attendees have lunch and dinner together for the purpose of socializing and sharing interests. Someone asked me how many children I had and I did not know how to answer the question—it was confusing. I said I had one child, a daughter, and I had had another child, a son, who was deceased.

But I was not at peace with that answer—it was just the best I could give to what to me was a very confusing question. When I returned home I shared this with Nancy. She got up from her chair walked over to me and held my face in both of her hands, looked deep into my eyes and said, "You have two children and you will always have two children."

It was an amazing gift of love, of clarity, of truth, and from that moment I have always felt the presence of my two children. I have felt closeness, connection and the unbreakable bond.

One of the parents I met who had lost his son to gun violence shared with me that it was important to not let the killer get into my head—that the killer had taken my son but to not let the killer also take my being. It was good counsel, and as of today I do not even know the killer's name. What I do know is that the killer is in jail and cannot come up for parole until he is 108 which means he will never do this to anyone else again.

I deliberately did not attend the killer's trial. I did write a letter that was read and is on file holding his parents responsible. He had been a child who had exhibited antisocial, aggressive and abnormal behavior, but rather than send him for treatment, the parents shunned him as they did not want their "reputation" soiled by having produced such a person. (This was information provided by the D.A.)

The killer led a nomadic life working as an itinerant construction worker along the West Coast and living in his van. It was that path that brought him to the restaurant where my son was that evening—an irreversible encounter that changed everything forever.

I spoke at Michael's memorial service and said that I would try to "soldier on" but I had no idea how to do it. Apparently, unconsciously, some part of me did, but I could not advise anyone how to be in touch with that part of human beings that can allow them to continue. It is all bewildering to me, and it always will be. Often when I look at Michael's picture while I say good night, I tell him that "I'm going to find you. I don't know where you are, but I'm going to find you." And I believe I will—and it gives me some comfort.

Elliot Fineman served as a strategic marketing consultant to Fortune 500 companies including top corporations like Accenture, KPMG and the Boston Consulting Group for 25 years. Following the murder of his son in 2006 by a paranoid schizophrenic who had legally obtained the gun, he founded National Gun Victims Action Council.

As a leading voice for a network of gun victims, survivors and the faith community seeing to change America's gun laws by adding an economic lever strategy, Mr. Fineman has appeared on CNBC, CNN, PBS, Fox News, the BBC, Al Jazeera English, Australian network TV and China Central Television (CCTV). He has been quoted by top media, like *USA Today*, National Public Radio, the *Chicago Sun-Times*, the *Morning Call* and written op-eds for the *Philadelphia Inquirer*, the *Times-Tribune* (Scranton), *Salem-News* (Washington State) and the *Capital Times* (Madison, WI.).

Trained at MIT as a civil engineer, Mr. Fineman is a skillful orator who has debated top-echelon NRA spokespeople on radio and TV and who addresses undergraduate and graduate students on the topic of gun violence at universities around the country.

Mr. Fineman served as host of NGVAC's bi-monthly radio show, "IT'S THE GUNS, STUPID", that aired on the AM station 1480 WPWC in Washington, D.C., reaching northern Virginia and southern Maryland, in 2014. The show, with well-known national guests, also reached nearly 600,000 social media members.

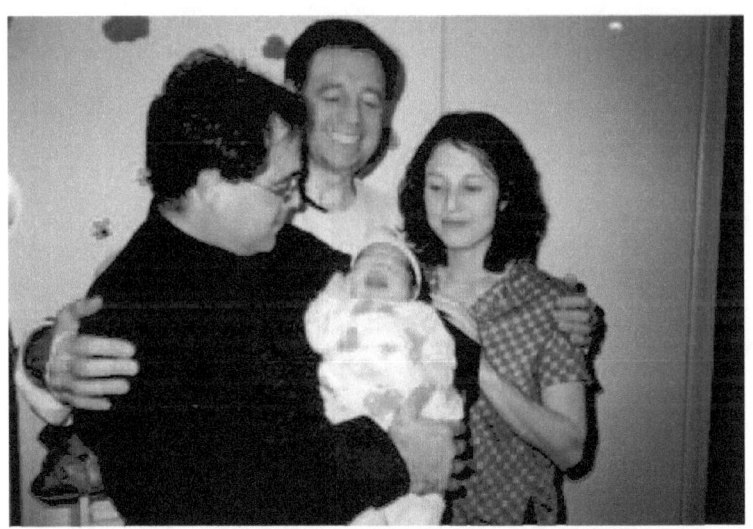

Elliot, Michael, Elissa and his granddaughter

Elliot Fineman

10

THAT FATEFUL DAY

ROSE PAGANO, PROVIDENCE, RHODE ISLAND

"The choice is not between violence and non-violence but between non-violence and non-existence."
~ *Rev. Martin Luther King*

It's been thirteen years and I still see the day of May 18, 2008, unfold in slow motion every day. It started out so beautifully—an early Mass, a May breakfast, and Louie's little league baseball game. My son, Lt. Jim Pagano, and his wife, Adriana, invited their immediate families to celebrate their son, Louie's, 9th birthday. So at 2 PM on that afternoon we all gathered at their home for our grandson's birthday party. Jim was a respected and dedicated 17-year veteran on the Cranston Fire Department. He was a loving and devoted husband and father of two beautiful children, a 9-year-old son and a 12-year-old daughter. We could not have asked for a more caring, considerate son.

A lovely day, all six of my grandchildren, ages 6 to 12, were playing ball outside on the cul-de-sac along with children from my daughter-in-law's family and other neighborhood children. Seeing so many children outside, an ice cream truck driver turned on to the cul-de-sac ringing his little bell. It was reminiscent of a Norman Rockwell scene. But then an errant tennis ball hit the neighbor's car and he came out screaming profanities at the children. When this was reported to my son, he went next door to admonish the neighbor for speaking to the children in such a way. After a heated argument, we suddenly heard shots being fired, saw my son running away, and children scattering. I (and all the young children playing outside) saw my son fall to the ground, shot in the back by the next-door neighbor on his son's 9th birthday.

At first, my brain didn't register what my eyes were seeing and my ears were hearing. Then I was in a state of shock and disbelief. Only after I heard my husband, who was with Jim at the neighbor's door, yell out, "You shot him," did I move into action to help my son. I ran to him despite the gunman holding his gun over him while he lay on the ground dying. I searched for a wound but couldn't find a gunshot wound because it went through his belt, so I started CPR to treat what I thought at the time may have been a heart attack caused by fear or running so fast. The gunman was still standing over Jim, my husband, and me pointing the gun at Jim. The CPR allowed Jim to sit up and say his final, reassuring words to me before collapsing, "I'm okay, I just need oxygen." The gunman finally left and my husband and I carried our son to the rescue unit because by that time we were surrounded by a SWAT team, which precluded the rescue team, that consisted of my son's brother firefighters and friends, from being allowed to come to him.

Words are inadequate to express what it's like to witness the murder of your son. It's something personal that only I and my husband will ever know and understand. Suffice it to say that it had a profound impact on our entire family who also witnessed the killing of our son, their devoted dad and husband, brother, uncle, and brother-in-law. We have learned the hard way that PTSD is very real and very debilitating. Since the senseless murder, our family has endured complicated grief, divorce, depression, anxiety, impulsivity and years of intensive counseling with intermittent success.

All our pain and the pain of the murderer's family could have been avoided had he not been allowed to automatically keep guns in his home simply because he was a "retired" police officer. He was only on the force for 1 and 1/2 years, only 6 months of that time on active police duty. After his so-called retirement he spent the following 15 years staying home building up a head of steam which finally blew on my son.

For me it's so simple. Take the gun out of the equation and my son and thousands of other loved ones would be alive today.

But here we are 13 years later. How did we get here? How did we cope with the myriad of issues that ensued after the trauma? Certainly the struggle is still on-going and the carnage we witnessed has become part of each of us and changed us for the remainder of our lives. There came a time, though, when I needed to make a choice. Did I want to live my remaining years despondent over what I lost; or did I want to live them grateful for what I had. Knowing very well what my son would have recommended for me, I made the conscious choice to be grateful, and I thank God every day for the blessings he has bestowed on me and my family. That decision, love of family and friends, and keeping busy are what got me through the most difficult time of my life.

Of course, I am grateful for my family—the love of a wonderful husband of 60 years, two beautiful daughters, my son, and six terrific grandchildren—my health, my faith, and my friends. But the gratitude I am speaking about goes much deeper, particularly with regard to our fateful day. My husband and I are so blessed to have had such a wonderful son for 44 years. In a heartbeat, I would take my son for 44 years over not having him at all. We are also extremely blessed that my son married so well. He married a woman who is kind, thoughtful, considerate and loving. She is a best friend to my two daughters, a daughter to my husband and me, and a loving and devoted mother to their two children. We had no fears, as others have experienced, of her keeping the children from us. In fact, to the contrary, she encouraged even more visits and respect. Their daughter, Adri, graduated from college in the spring of 2018 and their son, Louis, graduated from high school, proof that life goes on.

In a unique way we are blessed to be living in a small state because I believe that is an advantage to receiving swift criminal justice. Because Jim's murder was of great public interest locally, the murderer's trial was put on a fast track. A year after the murder, a jury trial was heard and my son's murderer was sentenced to 40 years (20 to serve) and a consecutive life sentence.

The incredible fact that we were all together and involved in some way with witnessing Jim's murder actually afforded my family an incomparable opportunity to talk to each other about their perceptions of what took place from their various vantage points. We talked and talked and talked and we are still talking and discovering new details. We all perceived that horrible event differently which gave rise to different outlooks and positions. For instance, my daughter deeply wishes that she did not witness Jim's death because she would rather remember him the wonderful way he lived his life as opposed to his final, sad day on earth. While I can certainly understand that, I, conversely, am so grateful that I was present. He said his final words to me. I was with him when he was born and I was with him when he died. Oddly, it also gives me comfort to know, unequivocally, all of the facts surrounding his murder exactly as they happened, leaving nothing to my imagination. Many loved ones are left wondering who, how, when, where and why their loved ones died. They can only imagine the horror their loved one may have experienced in their final minutes. At least I was there to comfort my son. I will accept repeatedly reliving that day over not knowing what took place because I definitely relive all the wonderful times in our lives as well.

Keeping my mind as busy as possible has certainly helped me to cope. Our son's life was senselessly cut short by gun violence. It seemed a natural progression to work toward preventing that kind of violence to try to make something good out of something so horrible. Sometimes things don't work out the way we imagine. I was recruited and urged to use our experience with gun violence to promote and encourage changes to our national and state laws in an attempt to limit the gun violence epidemic in America. This was a cause I supported even prior to Jim's murder. I must state that I am usually considered to be a very patient person, but this pursuit required a level of patience with legislators that I no longer possessed, at least with regard to this issue. It's simply beyond my comprehension why lawmakers do not easily pass laws that would save precious lives such as limiting the number of magazines in a clip or universal background checks. The inaction of lawmakers to pass common sense gun laws, particularly after the Newtown tragedy, caused me to have an unhealthy level of anxiety which I have been told may be a result of PTSD. The opposition's irrational and baseless arguments against any changes whatsoever were too much for me to tolerate. So for self-preservation, I needed to reduce those activities substantially, and withdrew emotionally from that issue. Does anyone really need an AK-47 or any assault rifle to protect themselves from intruders?

Our proudest accomplishment, though, is the Foundation my family formed in Jim's memory. Once the fog of grief lifted somewhat in 2011, we decided to establish a 501(c)(3) foundation and named it the Lt. Jim Pagano Foundation. Jim was deeply committed to improving the quality of life for citizens in the local community, especially children. It was with courage, confidence, passion and strong moral character that he lived his life, and it is the mission of the Lt. Jim Pagano Foundation to honor Jim's legacy and promote these esteemed values in children so they may thrive as adults. The Foundation makes charitable grants to individuals, groups and organizations that improve the quality of life for children, and foster character building and a strong foundation for their future. Our work is made possible by the generous contributions and involvement from the community.

We are proud to be able to say that over the past 10 years the Foundation has granted $175,000 to programs in academics, sports, arts, music and wellness. Among these funds are included five $1500 college scholarships each year and an after-school STEM Robotics program for 6th graders using Lego Minestorm.

We continue to be grateful to our community that supports the Lt. Jim Pagano Foundation each year. The work necessary for its fundraising efforts helps the family to cope with our loss by keeping us very busy while at the same time honoring our wonderful Jim.

So we count our blessings every day and continue to put one foot in front of the other to go forward. We all stumble once in a while, setting us back a little, which we consider ourselves to be normal after the trauma we all suffered in our lives. I miss my son more with each passing day, and I realize that will never change.

You may have noticed that throughout this statement I did not mention the name of my son's murderer and rarely use a masculine pronoun. I choose not to humanize or personalize the murderer in any way. Another coping strategy? Maybe.

A native of Westerly, Rhode Island, I studied court reporting for 2 years at Johnson & Wales University and in 1960 worked as a court reporter in the RI Superior Court. A few years later I left the position to raise my three children. Subsequently I took a position at Providence College and for 12 years created a verbatim record of its Faculty Senate meetings, transcribing from home in order to still be available for my children. I worked in a variety of part-time positions at the college until 1982 at which time I accepted the position of Senior Executive Assistant to the Vice President of Academic Administration and fulfilled that role until retirement in 2004. My son, Jim, was murdered in May, 2008 by an aggrieved neighbor, which prompted me to become active in Everytown Against Gun Violence and the local chapter of Moms Demand Action. Additionally, I serve on the Board of the Lt. Jim Pagano Foundation which grants funds to children in our local community in my son's memory.

Jim and son Louis as a baby

Jim and Adri

Adri, Jim's wife, Adriana, Louis and Jim

Jim, Louis as a baby, and Adri

Jim and his two sisters, Jean and Lisa

Jim with his mom and dad at promotion ceremony to rank of Lieutenant

Jim the fisherman

Jim's birthday

Jim and his mom at Lisa's wedding

Jim the watchful dad at Disney

Jim, Jean and Lisa

Jim

11

THE INDELIBLE DAY

ALVIN GLAZIER, ST. LOUIS, MISSOURI

"Good actions give strength to ourselves and inspire good actions in others."
~Plato

Life without our loved ones can feel like an insurmountable challenge.

I wrote this essay to share my experience and journey with a modern approach to loss. It lifted me from devastation to revelation.

This is my story:

The catastrophic nightmare of December 16, 2008 will be forever imprinted in my memory.

While driving, my cell phone rang. It was Susan's 18-year-old son, Daniel. He was in a state of panic and gasping for words. "I just got home…Mom's lying on the kitchen floor…she is unresponsive…and there's blood…what should I do?"

"Call 911 immediately. I'm on my way." I was scared to death.

Daniel's Mom, Susan was the love of my life.

Arriving at Susan's house in a state of shock, I was taken by a police officer to the back seat of a patrol car parked in the driveway. In the car, Daniel, his 16-year-old sister, Sarah and I were huddled, clinging together, frightened and trembling. With indescribable anxiety, we waited for what seemed like hours that cold, snowy afternoon.

When the paramedics and EMS finally emerged from the house, we broke down uncontrollably and knew our Susan had lost her life.

We were informed that more police, detectives and the Major Case Squad of St. Louis County were on their way.

I then made the most tragic, incomprehensible and frightening phone calls. The first, to Susan's parents in New York and the other to my sister, Lois who also lives in St. Louis.

Soon family and our closest friends arrived. Everyone gathered in an empty house across the street that was undergoing renovation.

About an hour later, Sarah, Daniel and I were driven to the Creve Coeur police station.

Our possessions were collected. The police finger-printed, separated and placed us in individual locked rooms. We were instructed to write where we had been and what we had done in detail that afternoon. Being considered a suspect was unimaginable during this terrifying ordeal, which lasted for six hours, finally ending at midnight.

With unbearable sorrow, disbelief and exhausted, we returned to my sister's house on this horrifying day.

Later, we learned Susan had returned home from shopping and within seconds encountered two 17-year-old burglars, one in possession of a stolen handgun, had broken into her home.

While trying to escape, she was brutally shot multiple times, in cold blood and died instantly.

The murderer and accomplice were quickly apprehended and jailed within 48 hours.

It took seconds to pull a trigger...but seemingly forever for justice to be delivered.

The judicial process dragged on for two painfully long years with two separate hearings, one for each of the accused. Both took "blind pleas," in which a defendant pleads guilty but not pursuant to any plea agreement between the state and the defense. A judge's blind plea sentence can be neither overturned nor appealed.

The self-confessed killer received a 50-year prison sentence, the accomplice, 20 years.

After the final hearing, the presiding judge said, "This is the most tragic, and sad case I have heard in my long career."

Susan was 48-years-old and grew up in Great Neck, New York. She was a loving mother, daughter, sister and my devoted partner.

She was a gifted and adored fitness professional, dancer and certified Pilates and Gyrotonic instructor who enhanced the lives of countless men and women of all ages. Her tragic loss profoundly affected the St. Louis and Great Neck communities.

In 2009, Dance St. Louis dedicated their January 23rd and 24th performances given by the Pilobolus dance group to Susan's life and memory.

We first met at a fitness center where I was a personal trainer and Susan was a member. With just one look, I was impressed by her exceptional fitness, posture and athleticism.

When she told me she was a triathlete, I asked, "Would you like to go biking sometime?" Our first date was a bike ride in the country, which surprisingly and excitedly led to dinner that evening...and a 13-year relationship. Her name was Susan—I referred to her as "Suze."

We instantly clicked. Our similar family backgrounds, sense of humor, interest in music, travel and careers as exercise professionals were strikingly evident. Maybe our meeting was predestined. Years later, Suze said her moving to St. Louis from New York was to meet me.

Susan was an extraordinary, unforgettable woman, a vibrant personality, a welcoming smile and always with grace and an outstretched hand.

The chemistry between us was undeniable. Whether on vacation or weekend trips, strangers would invariably ask, "Are you on your honeymoon?" Our reply, "Yes, of course." Was the relationship a fairy tale? No. We had our ups and downs, like any other couple. However, we lived and stayed together 13 wonderful, never-to-be forgotten years.

In our minds we were married, although not officially. Susan loved me more than anyone. As I did her.

I began saving for a surprise trip to Europe in celebration of Susan's 50th birthday. We talked about starting a fitness business in Mexico after her youngest graduated from college.

Our plans and life were destroyed by a gun.

Susan's heinous murder was incomprehensible. In an instant, our life together was obliterated. I was traumatized and sought professional help for the first time in my life. After a month of individual therapy, I felt something was missing. While searching and reading about other sources online, I discovered grief support programs.

A close friend of ours had met a grief-support director while visiting family in Chicago after Susan's funeral. The woman was a former director of the group I was considering. Whether by coincidence or fate, joining the Missouri Baptist Grief Support Group was life altering.

Prior to Susan's loss, I found that following my religious customs and practices after the deaths of my parents had failed to address my personal grief and mourning, which I had not learned.

I never realized my feelings were buried in my subconscious as "carried grief," until I found this grief support group in 2009.

The diversity of our group, which we called "Tuesdays at 11" only included spouses and partners. The group was comprised of varying ages, religions, backgrounds, people from different states and countries. Sharing their detailed stories, perspectives, progress made, tears and laughter was inspiring, encouraging and invaluable. The members quickly developed such a strong bond that will never be forgotten.

The "companioning" model put forth by Dr. Alan Wolfelt, was an integral part of my grief-support program. Instead of *treating* the bereaved, Dr. Wolfelt said, they should be *accompanied* on their grief journey.

I learned there is no clock, calendar or time limit on mourning and that grieving is heart-based, not intellectual nor academic. He explained that there are no definitive or linear *stages* of mourning—and how one feels about their grief—is their right.

Dr. Wolfelt wrote:

Reconciling loss is a journey through the wilderness of grief and the only way is straight through it. Grief is emotionally hard work and for some their greatest challenge. Grief and mourning are necessary for healing and reconciling loss.

Authentic mourning is an emotional and spiritual necessity, not society's view of weakness, flaws and self indulgence.

This focus on self-empowerment, dealing with death from the heart on one's own terms, was a new approach and right for me.

I was more prepared to face the first year of loss after reading the four extraordinary booklets of the Special Care Series by the late Doug Manning, bereavement author, grief counselor and advocate of companioning.

His words were like listening to a compassionate friend who had made this journey countless times, reassuring me---I could too. Allaying fear and anxiety, he walked with me throughout my unimaginable, difficult year.

His booklets were indispensable.

The unique help provided by the writings of these authors and my grief support group members enabled me to cope.

Being lost and a heartbroken soul, I gladly accepted my sister's offer to move into her home.

Living there for three months amounted to being thrown a life-preserver while I was treading water. My sister and brother-in-law lovingly kept me afloat.

My sister's home was the family meeting place. The presence of friends and close-knit relatives, especially my adored nieces and nephew, always lifted my spirit.

For the past 25 blessed years, Susan's children, her parents and brother have been family. Suze's inconceivable tragic loss has linked our hearts and bonded us together.

My special relationship with Susan's mother is responsible for my contribution to this book and her guidance has been invaluable.

Without the support of both families my journey would have been longer.

I have been an exercise professional for decades and know stress levels, anxiety and depression can improve with exercise.

My physical and emotional state crashed. Until it improved, returning to work or facing this horrific tragedy would be impossible.

Unlike physical work that recovers with rest, the emotional work of grieving causes a myriad of issues: lack of sleep, loss of concentration, energy and normal functioning. I had all of these, especially lack of sleep for many months.

Only after regaining my fitness and energy, did I seek help.

A big step forward toward healing was inspired by the power of nature. Six months after Susan's passing, I was hiking in the Inyo National Forest in California.

There in the "Dwelling Place of the Great Spirit," I felt a sense of calm and peace, unlike anything I had felt before. That sacred place brought me closer to my Suze, spiritually and literally at 11,000 feet.

My progress was made possible with the help of many.

The dedication and commitment of the Executive Director, Mary Schrader, M.A., her staff, interns and volunteers created a welcoming and safe environment conducive to sharing, learning and how to travel the difficult journey of reconciliation, moving forward in one's life. This was a most transformative experience.

I was ready to sign out of my group after two years. However, I remained to help others as those before me had done which was both beneficial for new members and myself.

After my departure from the group, I sent a letter to the Missouri Baptist Medical Center expressing my sincerest gratitude for their outstanding grief support program which helped countless people in St. Louis for many decades.

Although group support programs are not considered therapy, my group was for me just that and for many others. I hope those in crisis can find a miraculous program like I did.

No family should have to suffer the horror, sorrow and unending torment of gun violence. It is a cancer on our society, destroying lives and communities.

There are many excellent professional resources people can turn to for help in dealing with the loss of a loved ones. I hope they can find the right place for themselves and begin to move forward. I was among those fortunate enough to have done so.

In "Embrace the Memories," Doug Manning wrote:

> *In the early months of grief, memories brought tears and pain. In time, the memories that brought you the most pain will be the ones that bring you the most joy. You gradually move from the person being alive and present with you to the person having a new life in your memories and being with you in a new and different way. The memories gradually lead us to presence. Then we have our loved one in our hearts forever.*

It took years for me to find a new way to love Suze. When I did, I discovered that our life together was not gone. It was and is stored in my memory. Whenever and wherever, I can recall any moment or place we shared.

When I look at our hundreds of photos, they are not just pictures....I can envision and transport myself there, as though it were yesterday.

At times, I feel her presence and help, and she visits me in my dreams. Out of nowhere, a phrase, a word or a gesture of hers comes to me. She is, and always will be a part of me.

Susan (Suze) and Alvin

"We never lose our loved ones, nor our relationship
They're always with us,
We must remember and celebrate them.
The love emanating from my memories is eternal."

Martha Whitmore Hickman

Susan and Alvin

"We must remember the past, so we can sing in the present and dance into the future."

Dr. Alan Wolfelt

My participation in various organized sports began at a very early age, eventually sparking a lifetime interest in health and fitness. Many years later I became a certified personal trainer and gradually expanded my services by earning advanced certifications as a medical, corrective, functional and senior fitness specialist. Helping to improve the quality and longevity of life, is a most rewarding and satisfying career. I have been a certified and registered professional for 30 years. My life has been enriched by my cherished Suze and families.

ALVIN GLAZIER

12

MY "STORY," OR HOW I CAME TO BE PASSIONATE ABOUT GUN VIOLENCE

CHRISTINE ILEWSKI HUELSMANN, ST. LOUIS, MISSOURI

"If you can't fly, then run. If you can't run then walk. If you can't walk then crawl, but whatever you do you have to keep moving forward."
~Rev. Martin Luther King

On May 18, 2009, I woke up to a phone call. A close friend, Fr. Lorenzo (Larry) Rosebaugh, OMI (a Missionary Oblate Immaculate priest), had been gunned down in Guatemala. There was no apparent motive. The car he was driving with three other priests was stopped on the road and his life was taken in an instant. A life dedicated to social justice and the poorest of the poor was gone so quickly. He lived through the civil rights movement, hitchhiked and biked to South America several times, lived through civil wars, comforted and cared for countless poor. He had just turned 75 two days earlier. Gone so fast. Gone. Guns are so immediate.

Thirty five years ago, I got a similar phone call; my father had committed suicide, also by a gun. I was 20 and unable to process it. I shut down emotionally at the time. I remember going through the motions. Quickly packing a suitcase. Getting on a flight. Planning a funeral. Feeling very much out of my body, watching myself from a distance. Mostly thinking, I needed to get my younger sister, who had been visiting me at the time, to our Mom's arms. I was living in California with my husband and my dad had died in Missouri. He had also shot my stepmother. I knew he suffered from depression. He had been diagnosed as manic depressive at one point. Much later, I learned that he had been falsely accused of molesting his stepdaughter - a final trigger? He left no note, no explanation, although he wrote many long letters to his children over the years. He legally owned a handgun despite previous hospitalizations. It made for an easy impulsive decision that changed our lives forever. My sister was 16 and my brother was 14. My stepmother survived but was impaired and lost the custody of her two children.

The hardest part of writing this, even now, is lifting the "silence" rule "don't talk about it." It took years to speak about it. Only our closest friends and family know the story. It's not a topic of conversation. And I really hesitate now to tell this story that isn't just mine, but my siblings, my aunts and all those that loved my dad. There is such shame associated with suicide and gun violence in general. It only happens to "unstable" or "bad" people. Even the school shootings haven't really lifted the veil of blaming: "guns don't kill people. People kill people and it happens to 'other' people, in 'those' neighborhoods."

Only in this past year, with the help of a PTSD counselor did I finally realize that I blamed myself. So common, I'm told and so obviously inaccurate. But the mind does that after a trauma. Years of saying "of course it wasn't my fault" didn't erase the internalized message, a myth that somehow I knew something that would have prevented it from happening.

I remember going to a counselor shortly afterwards but just walking out of her office, unable to return. I really don't remember the first few months after he died. Time passed, I had my first daughter the following year. I divorced. I went back to school. I made art. I taught school. I remarried. I had twin daughters. My life seemed very full. The past way behind me until that morning, May 18, 2009.

My art work had always been "personal." I work from my center: my experience as a woman, a mother, a wife - a domestic, intimate life. In those recent years, I had focused on studies of my young daughters entering puberty - one struggling with a kidney disease. Occasionally, I stumbled into political content as in "King of Hearts, Power Puff Girl" in the Democracy Now exhibit at the Regional Arts Center, but I was oblivious of the bigger gun violence issue.

I often incorporated found personal objects, or painted on these objects. I have long been fascinated in the way we leave a bit of our spirit on the things we touch and how these things tell our story after we are gone.

Ultimately, the portraits of the "Faces Not Forgotten" project was begun.

Olivia Lahs-Gonzales, curator of the Sheldon Art Museum galleries, wrote about my work years ago: "Cheerful, vibrant colors belie underlying serious psychological issues that often have to do with interpersonal relationships."

But one "interpersonal relationship" I had never explored in my work was the sudden violent death of my father.

And I don't think I connected the Faces project to my Dad in the beginning at all. I just knew I wanted to do something to remember Lorenzo by, something to remember young lives lost so early because of gun violence. I had no idea of the numbers of young deaths there are. I know now. On average 8 a day age 20 and under, due to gun violence. I just did a portrait of one young man, William Jenkins, for his dad, Bill. I found his sweet face on-line in a blog his dad had made in his memory. I contacted Bill and asked if I could paint a portrait of William for him. His dad said "yes." I painted William in watercolor. The paint seemed to just flow into place, his eyes so bright and young. He seemed to come alive on the paper. He was 16 when he was gunned down in a robbery at the fast food restaurant he had just started working at. Afterward mailing it to Bill, I asked if it had given him comfort. And did he think other families would want a portrait. Bill said "yes" and helped me create a release form for families to submit photos of their loved ones that we still use today.

I painted more portraits of young gun violence victims for their families. I made the first copies on handkerchiefs by hand, "Faces Not Forgotten" and exhibited them in churches, galleries, a pop up exhibit in a U-haul I drove around St. Louis, Missouri and in marches honoring the children and protesting gun violence. It became emotionally exhausting to paint these young faces but I couldn't stop. A good friend, Jane Linders, saw my exhaustion and helped me find more artists to paint the portraits. We have a Board of Directors and expanded to other cities and states; Chicago, Texas, Georgia, New York City. We added others to our board who help with exhibits. The designer, Carol Luc, transforms photos of the portraits into the Faces Not Forgotten quilt panels we exhibit today - 8 tied together symbolic of the 8 young lives lost each day to gun violence. To date, we have completed about 120 portraits.

Do I wish sometimes that I had never started this? Honestly, I do. I am heartbroken with each story, each portrait we do. But I can't stop. These children are not just numbers or statistics. Each one of them has a "face" that I don't want forgotten. I travel with the exhibit and offer presentations to universities to educate young adults on the issue of gun violence. I want "Faces Not Forgotten" to have the name recognition some day that the AIDS quilts have. And I hope that with enough portraits completed and constantly exhibited, we can shine light on the elephant in the room, the deep horrific loss this country is experiencing due to gun violence. I hope that the very personal stories and images of these children will help legislators make sensible gun laws so that someday, we don't have to paint portraits. Meanwhile, I try to balance my life with other art work, paintings full of the spiritual stillness of nature, knowing that I am in this battle for the long haul. And I think of my dad a lot more often, as well as Lorenzo, hoping that their lives have gained meaning through this remembrance.

EXHIBITS/FURTHER THOUGHTS

SYRACUSE, New York – What does America value? Life or Liberty? *Deadlocked and Loaded: Disarming America* is a "locked and loaded" conversation through art, showcasing work in all media, that addresses our culture of violence and gun issues in the United States—particularly in how it affects women, children, and marginalized peoples. This exhibition, curated by Karen M. Gutfreund, is hosted across three galleries, in the first collaboration with artwork at ArtRage Gallery, Community Folk Art Center and Point of Contact Gallery in Syracuse, New York.

From a feminist perspective with artwork from 36 self-identified female artists with 52 works, this exhibition is an arresting, visual testimony combining lived experiences, memory, identity, and beliefs. It documents societal issues related to our culture of violence and systemic racism, crafting narratives blending art, activism, and a cry for social justice to amplify the voices of those who have been historically silenced.

Deadlocked and Loaded: Disarming America reflects this important cultural moment with art that shouts, "enough is enough" and speaks truth to power. This exhibition is meant to "disarm"—a double entendre—not only removing guns from society and those that would seek to harm, but more importantly, to be disarming to the viewer to engender empathy and compassion to the aftermath and consequences of violence.

"Thoughts and Prayers" is a phrase we hear used repeatedly as an expression of post-tragedy condolences—a hollow and meaningless platitude as a substitute for action against gun violence. We employ artwork to fight for human rights and social justice. "I created this exhibition because the subject matters are timely, necessary and urgently needed to be seen in a time of systemic racism, toxic masculinity, police brutality and the rise of white supremacy in America." says Gutfreund.

"Polarized, political times call for political, activist art and we are grateful for the opportunity to showcase these artists. ArtRage Gallery promotes and supports local, national, and global art activism. We believe that the artist's voice can help to foster important dialogues and inspire others to add their voice," says Rose Viviano, Executive Director and Co-Founder, ArtRage Gallery.

Given the volatile political climate, with the normalization of white nationalism and derisive rhetoric inciting violence, the last five years have made it clear there is a new urgency to address the root causes dividing the country. There is a troubling complacency to mass shootings at schools, churches and public spaces, shootings involving the police, and "stand your ground" ideology, all of which underscore the collective responsibility to come together for the health and wellbeing of our country, our communities, our families, and ourselves.

This exhibition seeks to engage viewers to listen to each other and collectively seek solutions. Art is a mirror we can hold up to look at ourselves. When we authentically come together, we are empowered to create community and facilitate positive change. We can alter the social narrative though art—it can influence the way we think and act as individuals, and as a society. We need the conversations and the actions that follow to build bridges to a more peaceable union that has the foundation of justice for all.

Deadlocked and Loaded was exhibited from February 11 to April 15, 2021. A full color catalog accompanied the exhibition and is viewable at:

https://issuu.com/home/published/deadlocked_and_loaded_disarming_america_issuu

Additional information including the curatorial essay, artist images and statements are available upon request.

Karen M. Gutfreund is an independent curator and artist. Actively promoting the work of activist and feminist artists with national touring exhibitions, she has produced over 35 to date, managing all aspects from curation, artist and project management, as well as the installation. Gutfreund has worked in the Painting & Sculpture Department at MoMA, the Andre Emmerick Gallery, The Knoll Group, the John Berggruen Gallery, and is an art consultant to corporations and individuals. Gutfreund served as the National Exhibitions Director for the Women's Caucus for Art. In addition, Gutfreund is a member of ArtTable, the Northern California Representative for The Feminist Art Project (TFAP), and curator for UniteWomen.org. She is currently writing a book on DIY Exhibitions. karengutfreund.com, @karengutfreundart

ArtRage: The ArtRage mission is to exhibit progressive art that inspires resistance and promotes social awareness; supports social justice, challenges preconceptions and encourages cultural change. Our goal is to provide ArtRage visitors with an experience that encourages the breakdown of boundaries so that people can see themselves in the work and then in one another. And that, we believe, is the seed of a movement for cultural and social change.

From its start, ArtRage has continuously partnered with community organizations in both exhibitions and exhibition-related- programming. The goal is always to bring attention to the meaningful work of local activists and organizations. To that end, all of our exhibitions are paired with exhibition-related programs such as films, lectures, workshops or theatrical productions that help to expand the dialogue created by each exhibition. artragegallery.org, @artragegallery

Community Folk Art Center: Community Folk Art Center, Incorporated (CFAC) was founded in 1972 by the late Herbert T. Williams, a professor in the African American Studies Department, in collaboration with other Syracuse University faculty and students, as well as local artists and Syracuse city residents. The primary motivation and objective for the establishment of CFAC was to provide a high-quality showcase for African Diasporan artists, creating a setting for dialogue and interaction among emerging, mid-career and professional artists, in Central New York. In addition to Williams, CFAC founders include Shirley Harrison, Jack White, George Campbell Jr., Mary Schmidt Campbell, David MacDonald, and Basheer Alim.

CFAC values our role as a vibrant cultural and artistic hub committed to the promotion and development of artists of the African Diaspora. CFAC's mission is to exalt cultural and artistic pluralism by collecting, exhibiting, teaching and interpreting the visual and expressive arts. Public programming includes exhibitions, film screenings, gallery talks, workshops and courses in studio and performing arts. A proud unit of the African American Studies Department at Syracuse University, CFAC is a beacon of artistry, creativity and cultural expression engaging the Syracuse community, the region and the world. CommunityFolkArtCenter.org, @communityfolkartcenter

Point of Contact Gallery: Punto de Contacto/Point of Contact, Inc., a New York-based arts organization in residence at Syracuse University, creates opportunities for the exploration of diversity and the exchange of ideas through the verbal and visual arts. Working with the Central New York communities, as well as state-wide and international institutions and individuals, Point of Contact is a collaborative, cross-disciplinary forum where artists, writers, scholars and students actively engage in the production of publications, art exhibitions and events to enrich the cultural mix of our society. Our organization aims to form inspired communities, to innovate through artistic concepts that may resonate locally and globally, to work expansively where intellectual and geographic boundaries are concerned, and to share the experience.

Point of Contact, Inc. is a (501c3) tax-exempt organization. The organization's headquarters are housed at Syracuse University's Warehouse Building in downtown Syracuse. Point of Contact is supported by grants from Syracuse University's College of Arts and Sciences, the Coalition of Museum & Art Centers at Syracuse University (CMAC), and the New York State Council on the Arts. Point of Contact is managed by the Office of Cultural Engagement for the Hispanic Community in the College of Arts and Sciences at Syracuse University. puntopoint.org, @pointofcontactgallery

Reverend Lorenzo Rosebaugh

John Ilewski

MY "STORY," OR HOW I CAME TO BE PASSIONATE ABO... | 121

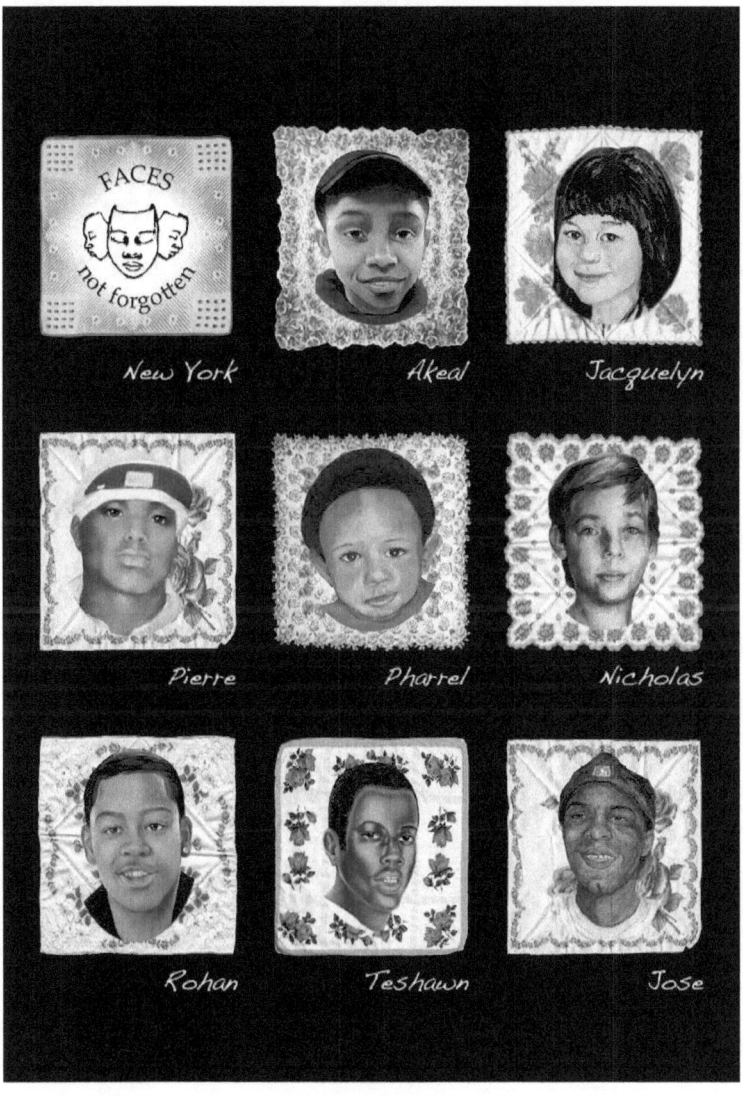

"Faces Not Forgotten"

OBLATE COMMUNICATIONS PHOTO
The Rev. Lorenzo Rosebaugh, who lived most of his life in Third World countries, had planned to return here to retire.

Activist Catholic priest loved working with poor

The Rev. Lawrence Rosebaugh, murdered Monday in Guatemala, had St. Louis roots.

BY TIM TOWNSEND • ttownsend@post-dispatch.com > 314-340-8221

Before he was murdered on Monday in Guatemala, the Rev. Lawrence Rosebaugh, had received permission from his religious order to retire in his hometown of St. Louis.

"He wanted to come back was what the 74-year-old Rosebaugh's life was about. For most of that life, the priest — a member of the Missionary Oblates of Mary Immaculate — was more comfortable in the poor areas of Brazil or

Christine Ilewski Huelsmann

13

SANDY AND LONNIE PHILLIPS

ON THE ROAD IN AN RV

Nonviolence is the greatest force at the disposal of mankind. It is mightier than the mightiest weapon of destruction, devised by the ingenuity of man.

~ Mahatma Gandhi

We are Sandy and Lonnie Phillips, ordinary Texas citizens, but the ordinary became an extraordinary story regarding our daughter, Jessi, and we all became gun violence victims on several levels.

July 19, 2012 began like any other ordinary day. The only thing out of the ordinary was the publicity throughout the country. It was the premiere of the "The Dark Knight Rises."

It was a "hot" ticket and the anticipation for the screening of the film ran high for many people. Our daughter Jessi was one of those people. She shared the thrill she felt with us about seeing the film because she loved the character and the series and was scheduled to see a midnight screening at that theater in Aurora.

On that catastrophic evening, 70 people were injured, 12 people were killed and our beloved Jessi was one of the victims who was brutally murdered by gun fire. The massacre was the largest recorded number of casualties in a shooting until the Orlando massacre four years later.

It is strange to note that one month prior, Jessi survived a mall shooting in Toronto, Canada.

Jessi's given name was Ghawi although professionally she was known as Redfield. Perhaps we could conclude that the "red" in her name was purposefully taken to emphasize her vibrancy, an unbounded zest for life which also matched her red hair.

She was fun, funny and sharp-witted. Multiple times we were told that Jessi captured the respect of whoever she came into contact with. She aspired to be the best she could be and therefore became an inspiration to others.

Her passions were journalism/blogging and sports, and her favorite sport was hockey. At 24 years of age she had a promising media career which combined her love for sports and journalism.

Jessi grew up in Texas but traveled to Colorado to begin her multifaceted career as an intern at a Denver radio station, covering the Colorado Avalanche hockey team while also studying broadcast journalism at Metropolitan College.

After the Toronto shooting, Jessi wrote in a blog: *"I was shown how fragile life was. I saw lives change. I was reminded that we don't know when or where our time on Earth will end. When or where we will breathe our last breath...I say all the time that every moment we have to live our life is a blessing. So often I have taken it for granted."*

I have a vivid recollection of that horrendous evening. I was asleep in the bedroom. Sandy couldn't sleep and was in the living room when the call came. The sound of her scream was so piercing and agonizing that I thought she was being attacked by an intruder.

We are gun owners and I immediately thought about the unloaded shotgun that I kept in my closet. But there was no time to load a shotgun. I had to get to my wife.

I found her sliding to the floor with her back against the wall screaming Jessi is dead. In that instant that I heard her scream those words that no parent should ever hear, I knew that I no longer had a daughter and my wife would never be the same.

We became "accidental activists" a few weeks after Jessi's Memorial. We went on national television and asked the question; "How can any person go online and buy thousands of rounds of metal piercing bullets without a background check?" We wanted to know why AR-15's and .223 ammo were so easily available to the public. Just five months later, Sandy Hook happened and those questions were asked again...by lots of people. Both the public and the gun violence prevention organizations wanted answers and wanted change.

We did not know it at the time, we were so naive. But it was very clear to the top two gun violence prevention organizations that the emotional and authentic voices of survivors of gun violence are valuable assets. The horror of the Aurora massacre on July 20th and then the slaughter of 20 babies and 6 educators at Sandy Hook, unleashed an unseemly competition and a round of exploitation that remains invisible to people outside, and many inside of the gun violence prevention movement today.

It is a fact of life that even the best and most altruistic public service organizations compete for funding. We discovered that the two major national gun violence prevention groups were hunting and competing fiercely for gun violence survivors and victim's family members, like us.

These two giant groups utilized any human assets they could recruit and then have them participate in media events tied closely to fundraising appeals.

The Brady organization asked for our help at a press conference in Washington, D.C. We were to appear in front of the international press along with Brady's president. After several days of appearances, while the three of us relaxed over drinks, the president of Brady offered Sandy a job. A few weeks later, I was hired as The Brady Campaign Manager for Gun Owners.

We were thrilled. Brady had a ten year plan to reduce gun violence by 50% and they were making us a part of it. We left our old jobs believing we were part of something that would save lives and take us into retirement.

It was during the honeymoon period of our early days that the Brady lawyers asked us to join their plan to overturn a perverse federal law known as the Protection of Lawful Commerce in Arms Act (PLCAA). Brady wanted us to sue the gun manufacturer Lucky Gunner (which does business as "Bulk Ammo" online), and the other online sellers that sold the ammunition, tear gas, body armor and 100-round magazines to the shooter who killed our daughter.

No other survivors or victims of the Aurora Theater shooting would join this federal lawsuit because they were concerned about their own financial liabilities. We trusted that Brady would honor their verbal promise to have our backs if the lawsuit was dismissed or failed.

When we decided to "go it alone," we wanted it made clear to the judge that we were doing this for the purpose of getting rid of this egregious law and not for financial gain. We sued Lucky Gunner just to get them to change their reckless business practices. All we wanted was for them to agree to act in a more responsible way. We wanted to show them a safer way to sell dangerous armaments, a way that could help to prevent another tragedy like Aurora.

Only in the topsy-turvy world of American gun laws could victims of gun violence be forced to suffer financially for seeking non-monetary justice.

We were hired by Brady in January, 2013. We were unceremoniously dismissed on December 12, 2014, almost 90 days after Brady "led" the federal lawsuit against Lucky Gunner.

Six months after our dismissal from Brady the "final" blow landed. On June 17, 2015, the federal judge assigned to our Brady lawsuit threw us right out of court without letting us speak. So far, our former employer has been a no-show in the aftermath.

Our legal system interpreted the laws passed by our congress and gave the gun industry a pass and ordered us, "the victims," to pay $203,000 to Lucky Gunner for attorney's fees. Lucky Gunner pledged that any money received from us would be distributed among the most prolific gun-lobbying organizations. In other words, they were going to use our money to fight us and our mission to make gun violence a public health issue.

How could this have happened to us? How did we go from an ordinary middle-class couple grieving for our beloved daughter to a desperate pair, unemployed and hounded into bankruptcy? As victims we were further victimized.

A friend once said to me, "Money worries are oppressive. They are a dark cloud, always there, always lurking, waiting in the background to take over everything in your life." Truer words couldn't have been spoken.

We filed for bankruptcy on January 27, 2017, the day after I celebrated my 73rd birthday. Bankrupt and battered, we began to reflect.

We want to make it clear, if it were not for the good works of all of Brady's local chapters and hundreds of other local and state grassroots organizations all over the country like Colorado Ceasefire, Women Against Gun Violence, New Yorkers Against Gun Violence, States United, Moms Demand Action and many, many others too numerous to name that make up 90% of the boots on the ground, we would not have the support or the stamina to continue this fight.

These are the people we love. It is all the victims and survivors of gun violence working with other compassionate volunteers and dedicated groups who are making things happen at the state level. Most of them have been in this fight much longer than we have. They are truly the ones who do the heavy-lifting. These are our heroes.

We have become nomads, traveling from state to state fervently trying to fight gun violence in our new home—a used camper.

Our organization survivorsempowered.org is developing personal relationships with gun violence survivors across the country. We still work collaboratively with other national groups in the gun violence prevention community like Coalition to Stop Gun Violence (CSGV), Giffords, Sandy Hook Promise, Newtown Action Alliance, Change the Ref and Guns Down America. We combine expertise and resources when possible . We are creating a platform "by survivors, for survivors, empowering survivors" that will allow gun violence survivors a safe place to speak in their own authentic voice and drive change, both in terms of policy and by redefining our national debate about guns in their individual states.

These last nine years have been difficult. It is not easy to start over at our ages and to face each day without our daughter. June, 2013 was the first year without our daughter. It was especially difficult because it was Father's Day and the airing of the Alex Jones interview with Megyn Kelly. On Father's Day the year before she was killed, Jessi posted a photo of us on her Facebook page. It was a photo that Sandy took when Jessi was five years old. That photo of Jessi lying asleep on my chest while I was asleep in the rocking chair captured Jessi's confidence in our relationship ... she knew that she was safe with me.

She chose that photo and chose this caption to tell me how strong our bond was.

"Bubba, Thank you for teaching me how to laugh, how to love and how to throw a punch...I love you."

As her Bubba, SHE is the only one I answer to. SHE is the one I "fight" for, SHE is the reason that I have no fear when I stand nose to nose with Alex Jones and trade spittle with him after he tells my wife to her face that our Jessi never existed, that we are paid actors, and that the massacre that happened in that Aurora Theater was a "false flag."

SHE is why we can continue to fight on...Broke and broken, but far from weak and still throwing punches!

Sandy and Lonnie Phillips are the parents of Jessica Ghawi who was murdered in the massacre at the midnight showing of the "Dark Knight Rises" in July, 2012 in Aurora, Colorado. They believe gun violence is a public health and safety issue and they speak about prevention and how to take action by forming coalitions with other grassroots groups. In the nine years since the death of their daughter, Sandy and Lonnie have been on the ground in the immediate aftermath of seventeen public mass shootings. They have created a non-profit organization, "Survivors Empowered" that will empower gun violence survivors a safe place to speak in their own authentic voice.

Jessi at 5 years old and Lonnie.

Lonnie and Sandy Phillips

Sandy and her daughter, Jessi Ghawi

14

GUNS AND A HEART OF FLESH

RABBI SHAUL MARSHALL PRAVER, NEWTOWN, CONNECTICUT

"Justice is truth in action."
~ Benjamin Disraeli

It was a tragic destiny to be one of the spiritual "first responders" at the Sandy Hook Elementary School shooting in Newtown, Connecticut, on December 14, 2012. I was the rabbi of Congregation Adath Israel. Denomination was irrelevant as we did what little we could do to comfort traumatized families.

Two days later, destiny brought me in the presence of President Obama on national television to intone the Hebrew memorial prayer. For a number of reasons, the shooting at Sandy Hook Elementary School was the tipping point and Newtown turned into more than an "effect" but a "cause." Our mantra became "Newtown shall no longer be remembered as the town of the tragedy, but the bridge to a new and kinder world." Fulfillment of this cause is the only way we know how to quiet the cries from so much bloodshed.

I am haunted to this day by the memory of six-year-old Noah Pozner, one of twenty children murdered at Sandy Hook, in his coffin. An inner voice wailed, "Is this the boy once filled with mischievous pranks and eyes glowing? No! This is only an effigy of the lad who has moved to a world worthy of his innocence."

Since that time, I have devoted much of my life substantially addressing violence and incivility in the country. My book, *The Love Zap*, is my official response to this historic massacre. In my new role as author and facilitator of civil dialogue, I listen to all perspectives, ranging from those who advocate robust gun regulation to those who propound sacrosanct gun rights. I discovered that all people shed tears in equal measure for innocent victims of gun violence.

I was privileged to participate in a screening of Abigail Disney's documentary film, *Armor of Light*, in Newtown, in which my colleague and friend, Evangelist Reverend Robert Schenck, is featured and who, along with Abigail Disney, attended the screening and participated in the structured dialogue.

The conversations were spirited and civil and led us all to conclude that guns—gun violence, gun regulations and gun rights—are only the tip of the iceberg. Our hearts need a whole new way of being. Passing laws before changing hearts is like scattering seeds before plowing the field. Just as the field must be turned over, so must the heart. While civil dialogue will not deliver goods and services instantly upon demand, it will prepare hearts for needed change. It brings to mind Ezekiel 36:26-27:

".... I will give you a new heart and put a new spirit within you, and I will remove your heart of stone and replace it with a heart of flesh."

My conservative colleague and friend, Ralph Benko, who participated, reported, "We did not unravel the Gordian knot, but we broke through the dogmatic logjam. That's powerful. It's where solutions come from."

Writer Carol Ascher, who attended our Newtown screening of *Armor of Light*, shared her impressions:

> "With the NRA creating a stalemate in Washington, Rabbi Praver and Reverend Schenck suggest that spiritual communities around the country need to take responsibility for a new kind of conversation about gun safety one that is faith-based,' features personal stories, and is respectful and empathic.
>
> *As I leave the church, I take to heart Rabbi Praver's admonition to listen carefully to those whose views differ from ours:* "Never assume, as a liberal, that conservatives shed fewer tears over gun violence."

What causes our lack of empathy? Dogma. Dogmatism's emphatic—sometimes borderline fanatic—nature leads us to believe we are in exclusive possession of truth. Dogma deafens us to those who share our goals but dispute our preferred means.

At the end of the day, good, old-fashioned heart-to-heart conversations conducted in a spirit of respect is our best way forward. If we could spark off a massive return to this paradigm, we really could transform the tragedy of Sandy Hook into a bridge to a new and kinder world. We really could reach a historic agreement and draft a new social contract with guns in America, and we really could birth a culture of peace---worthy of the Sandy Hook families and us all.

Shaul Marshall Praver was ordained as a Rabbi by the Jerusalem Rabbinate in 1989, is a Board Certified Chaplain through the Association of Professional Chaplains, earned his Doctor of Ministry through Hartford International University, was elected Senior Fellow at the Dietrich Bonhoeffer Institute in Washington, D.C. and the former "Newtown Rabbi" who served as a spiritual first responder at the mass shooting at the Sandy Hook Elementary School on December 12, 2012. Rabbi Praver became known to many when he co-officiated the memorial service with his colleagues from the Interfaith Group together with President Barack Obama on Sunday, December 16, 2012 at the Newtown High School.

Shortly after the shooting, Rabbi Praver left the pulpit and began serving as a correctional chaplain in Connecticut's state prisons. Newsweek recognized Rabbi Praver as one of the 50 most influential rabbis of the year in 2013 for his spiritual leadership. He also worked with PICO (Pacific Institute for Community Organizations) ensuring that 4000 faith communities endorsed the Newtown Clergy Letter calling upon the nation and its government to take practical steps toward ending rampant gun violence. Rabbi Praver advocated for a culture of peace and civility on nearly every major television, radio and print venues in the country including, CNN, MSNBC, NPR, the New York Times, Politico, Newsday, Boston Globe, as well as Israel's Jerusalem Post and Ha'aretz. Rabbi Praver was awarded the prestigious Samaritan Medal for Peace and Humanitarian Achievement in 2013 and the Yuval award from the Cantors Assembly.

Praver ran unsuccessfully for U.S. Congress in Connecticut's 5th district in 2016, and spoke out forcefully in Waterbury and Newtown when Mexican children had been violently separated from their parents at the nation's southern border and Muslims were banned from entering or reentering the country. Rabbi Praver's spiritual presence has reached people from every faith, race, class and political ideology. He believes the world needs transcend love to heal its wounded heart.

GUNS AND A HEART OF FLESH | 139

Rabbi Shaul Marshall Praver and House Speaker Nancy Pelosi

Rabbi Shaul Marshall Praver

In Memorium

15

OUR HEARTS ARE BROKEN

RISA ZWERLING WRIGHTON, ST. LOUIS, MISSOURI

"Those who make peaceful revolution impossible, make violent revolution inevitable."
~John F. Kennedy

Chelsea Harris, a 16-year-old junior in high school, was gunned down and murdered on a residential street last week in south St. Louis. Yes, the police have caught the gunman. The case has already become yesterday's news.

Has justice been served? Well, I guess as much justice as we can expect in a state and country that refuses to get guns off the streets. The police risk their lives every day tracking down assailants and packing them into prisons. And our children risk their lives every day, walking home from school and sitting on their front porches because Americans and our legislative representatives value the right to bear arms over the lives of our children.

We are a great country in many, many ways, but we are sacrificing our right to life, liberty and the pursuit of happiness for the many who live in poor, underserved communities riddled with hopelessness and the crime that ensues. Any criminal can find a weapon. We don't make it very hard.

My heart is broken. I knew Chelsea since she was 9 years old and loved her. I became her mentor for a number of years through an organization called Discovering Options. I got to ride some of the ups and downs of raising this beautiful girl. I became close with her great-grandmother, Vernell Williams, who was her legal guardian and worked tirelessly to protect and care for Chelsea. Mrs. Williams was able to get Chelsea into the Lift for Life Academy, where she was nurtured and supported through the tumult and pain of adolescence and her early teenage years.

At school, there wasn't a day that went by where Chelsea wasn't given a hug and encouragement and a platform to learn. Chelsea started to embrace her education and was getting good grades in recent years. She was talking about going to college. She would be the first person in her family to do so. That's not going to happen now.

She had a right to live her life in safety and in the pursuit of happiness. And in the words of songwriter Joni Mitchell, she will never again awake to a "Chelsea Morning, where the first thing that she knew. There was milk and toast and honey and a bowl of oranges, too. And the sun poured in like butterscotch and stuck to all her senses."

My heart is broken not only because of Chelsea but because of all the Chelseas out there who won't feel the sun on their faces anymore. There are many factors that contribute to violence in our communities and we have to work on them all but we can't get any traction until the guns are gone. Rep. Stacey Newman, (D) Richmond Heights, has dedicated much of her legislative career to bringing gun control laws to our Legislature, and the bills languish. Her most recent bill, House Bill 187, hasn't even come to the floor for discussion.

If momentum to make substantive change in our gun control laws came and went with Sandy Hook Elementary and the shooting of U.S. Rep. Gabby Giffords, what kind of impact can the killing of 16-year-old Chelsea Harris possibly have? What is finally going to make a difference? I don't know. I'm endlessly sad. Chelsea was buried this week.

(This article appeared in the St. Louis Post Dispatch in December, 2014. Permission to reprint this article was given by Risa Zwerling Wrighton and the Post Dispatch.)

Risa Zwerling was raised in New York City and attended Barnard College, where she received a Bachelor of Arts (AB) in Psychology in 1970. She received her Master's of Social Work (MSW) from the University of Maryland in 1975 and a Master's in Business Administration (MBA) from Washington University in 1989. Ms. Zwerling combined both her social work and business experience at Magellan Behavioral Health where she developed mental health and work /life balance programs for large corporate employers to assist them in maintaining healthy workforces. She retired from Magellan in 2007.

In 2007, Ms. Zwerling became a 4-year academic advisor at Washington University where her husband served as Chancellor from 1995 to 2019. She is the founder of Home Plate, where, each year, she places hundreds of students with local families for a "touch of home away from home." In 2015, she and her husband spearheaded Washington University's year-long gun violence prevention initiative to address gun violence as a public health crisis. This project has led to the establishment of the St. Louis Area Violence Prevention Commission to continue this effort. Ms. Zwerling is currently on the boards of Our Little Haven, Provident, Inc., and has been involved in mentoring disadvantaged youths. In 2018, Ms. Zwerling was named a Woman of Achievement for Impactful Leadership in the St. Louis region. Ms. Zwerling looks forward to continuing her involvement with Washington University as she and her husband explore life after leading the university.

Ms. Zwerling is the proud mother of two daughters and four granddaughters – unequivocally her proudest accomplishment.

Mark Wrighton, Chancellor Emeritus of Washington University, St. Louis, Missouri. Currently he is the James & Mary Wertsch Distinguished Professor at Washington University.

A younger Chelsea

Chelsea Harris

Risa Zwerling Wrighton

Mark Wrighton and Risa Zwerling Wrighton

16

A SHORT STORY OF BECCA

MARLENE ELDEMIRE, MAINEVILLE, OHIO

"You don't spread democracy with the barrel of a gun."
~ Helen Thomas

Lois and I met at a concert against gun violence in New York City. We're both grieving mothers who lost daughters to gun violence. Our stories are horrific, unimaginable, and beyond comprehension. Lois asked me to write a few words about my daughter. The next thing she asked of me was a gift I don't think even she realizes she gave to me. Lois asked me to write about the daughter I wanted her and you to know. She said while it's important to tell the ugly part of their story, she really wants people to learn the beauty of Becca, which is her life.

REBECCA CASEY ELDEMIRE.

There are many adjectives I've heard used when describing Becca. Smart, soulful, beautiful, sassy, game changer, wise, loud, sincere, loyal, sweet, bold, brave, strong, funny and many more. I think of her as the wide-eyed, full of wonderment, bouncy, laughing girl with a head full of untamable curls. She was the girl wearing a perfectly pink frilly, lacy dress, and hiking boots on her feet. There was no room for pretension in Becca's personality. What you saw is what you got.

I remember dinner at a friend's house when Becca was a toddler. Our friend so lovingly and graciously put a jungle animal themed plate of food on Becca's tray. From her throne, actually highchair, Becca took a taste of the food, and with wrinkled nose, pursed lips, eyes squinting in disgust, picked up the plate, yelled "Yuck, hate this!" and threw all of it on the floor.

No bullshit! That pretty much sums up Becca. I could tell you how smart she was, how gorgeous and thoughtful, and how outspokenly protective of what or whom she loved. However, I think the Becca she would want you to know is with her: there was no bullshit! Something I'm so proud of as her mother.

While on a trip to Africa with a college group Becca's unnerving tenacity served her and the other six girls quite well. Every morning and afternoon they walked 4 miles each way on a dusty, dry road from their host home to the primary school in Maji ya Chai where they taught English to young children. One particular morning a van showed up at the school with some rather large, burly, not particularly friendly men to tell Becca and her friends they didn't have the proper visas to teach in Tanzania. The girls were taken through a back door of the police station to a stark interrogation room. This group of seven beautiful, seemingly naïve college girls were told to each pay $200 cash to get the "visa thing" sorted. What these crooked criminals didn't know was before them stood a 19 year old girl from Ohio who was an outspoken champion of the underdog with a propensity for not backing down. After many hours, phone calls home, steely determination, a few tears and a call from the US Embassy, the crooks ran away. Literally. When the call came from the US Embassy in Dar es Salaam the standoff ended with the coward crooks running out of the police station and seven girls with their wallets intact.

There are many stories of Becca's fierce protection and compassion for all those she loved including animals, the environment, human rights, her friends and family.

Becca's brother is 3 years older and a lot more timid than his sister. Admittedly, there were some fast food dinners at those places with indoor playgrounds in the early years. Josh happily ate a greasy meal that came with the cool toy while Becca dined on her favorite, salad with ranch dressing. Like clockwork, Josh drank his soda rather quickly. He waited until his little sister noticed his empty cup, laid her fork in her salad, grabbed him and his cup by the hand, marched them to the counter she could barely see over from tippy toes, and loudly asked for a soda refill for her "bruhver". He was five, she was two.

To say she was a force with which to be reckoned is an understatement. Becca accomplished much in her too brief life on earth. She was an honors student, artist, regular volunteer at the animal shelter, historian of her college honor fraternity, summer intern at an organic farm, world traveler, sandwich artist at Subway, engineer school librarian and so much more.

Becca was my daughter and my best friend. Life without her is excruciatingly painful. This profound hole in my heart will never mend yet her beautiful eternal spirit lives on in everyone who had the good fortune to know her.

On February 1, 2015 at 21 years of age, Becca was murdered while sleeping by two gun shots to the face by the boyfriend she broke up with 24 hours earlier.

#Becca4Ever

. . .

To LEARN MORE about Becca please visit BEEPSFoundation.org, the nonprofit established to carry on her beautiful legacy.

Marlene Eldemire's daughter, Becca, was murdered 24 hours after breaking up with her boyfriend. He shot her twice in the face. Following Becca's brutal death, Marlene struggled to find a reason to go on with her own life.

She found love and comfort through newly gained friendships in the gun violence survivor community.

She is the Executive Director of The BEEPS Foundation, Betterment for Environmental & Earth Protection. The foundation is an extension of Becca's dedication to the care and nurturing of our planet, people and animals. Beeps was also Becca's nickname. (You can read more at beepsfoundation.org)

Marlene is a wife, mother and grandmother. She lives in Ohio with her husband and 3 cats.

Marlene Eldemire

Marlene Eldemire with a photograph of her daughter, Becca

REFLECTION

TRENELLE GABAY, BROOKLYN, NEW YORK

"The ultimate measure of a man is not where he stands in the moments of comfort and convenience but where he stands at times of challenge and controversy."

~ Rev. Martin Luther King

"I found Love. I imagined it. I visualized it to come. We met. He chased me and I caught him. He peeled down walls until I started to fall in love with him. His words, "if you fall I will catch you." He was a poet in his own right. I used to say to him, "you always have the right words to say Mr. Gabay" and there I was in Love.

What I miss. His warm, alluring, playful, coy smile. His enticing, bright, intense eyes. His deep, sonorous, passionate voice. When we held hands I would feel his strength flow right through me. His gentle kisses on my forehead consumed my thoughts with the constant feeling of security. Hearing the beating of his heart as he slept while my head moved on his chest from his breath. Calling him happy feet as both of our competitive natures would lead us to the dance floor when we heard a dope beat. The list of missing can go on for a lifetime because You are the one that is missing."

I commemorate the memory of You my dear husband on what would have been your 45th birthday. Turning the headline of tragedy to a recollection of the life you lived and lives that you continue to inspire and touch in spirit."

With loving memories always and forever, your wife,

Trenelle Gabay

On September 7, 2015 my beloved husband, Carey Gabay was shot. Carey was 43 years young and I had to watch my husband fight for his life for 8 days as he laid in a coma. On September 15, 2015, one of the hardest, darkest decisions of my life was upon me and that was to take my husband off of life support as he was pronounced brain dead.

Thoughts of my husband continually reverberate throughout my body and soul as he is missed every minute of the day. I wrote "REFLECTION" on his 45th birthday. I wanted to keep him in my heart while displaying our magnetic chemistry, attraction and love.

My husband was Assistant Counsel to our Governor of New York, Andrew Cuomo. What is ironic is Carey helped to draft legislation for the SAFE ACT which set precedence for sensible gun ownership in New York State. However, Carey became a victim and so did I.

Every year in Brooklyn there is an annual celebration called the Labor Day Parade or West Indian Carnival, which happens on the first Monday in September, the parade attracts millions of participants. On display are beautiful costumes and rhythmic sounds of music. Before the opening of the parade the actual start of carnival is a pre-dawn street festival called J'Ouvert which in French means daybreak. Carey left our home alongside his brother and friends to take part in his heritage by partaking in J'Ouvert which is characterized with camaraderie and joyousness indicative of our rich West Indian heritage. But on this particular day instead of a celebration, it became a day of horror, shock, mourning, sorrow and heartbreak.

As Carey walked down the street with his brother and friends two rival gangs were in a shootout. As they ran and ducked for cover, Carey was caught in between the crossfire and fatally shot in the head.

Carey and I shared intense pride in our culture. I am of Trinidadian decent; Carey was of Jamaican decent and together we shared the joy of participating in this celebration. I now view that time of year as heartache instead of jubilance.

When I first heard of the shooting, the phone rang after 3 a.m. It was my mother-in-law praying at the other end. Her exact words were "My daughter, Carey was shot and he is dead." I remember screaming out MOM ... What ... and when she repeated those words I screamed NO and then fainted. As I woke with intense pain, screaming, crying and shaking I began to pray. *Dear Lord my husband is alive, he MUST be alive, please keep him alive.* My second phone call was, "Your husband is alive and fighting, get to the hospital." As I got in a cab I was in disbelief—how could this happen? NO, this is not happening. I was in shock. All of a sudden I began to tremble and I was overcome with pain and sorrow that enveloped my body combined with extreme anger. I was confused, I was heartbroken and the tears were endless. Who could ever imagine that this would happen, devastation and a complete emotional upheaval.

Walking into the hospital and seeing my husband lay there the emotions are impossible to explain. There was a darkness of despair and for the first time in my life I felt helpless. The news of gun violence was being broadcasted daily and I never thought that I could be a victim. With each passing day of my husband fighting for his life I kept hoping and praying that he would live, but with each passing day it became apparent that all hope was fading. Everyday my husband's health was depleting and he was slowly dying.

Every day I prayed for a full recovery and if not a full recovery anything—Lord, just don't take my beloved away. My prayers were not answered. I had to plan a funeral and bury my husband at 37 years young. At Carey's funeral Governor Cuomo stated, "This was a beautiful man, a sweet man, a man who was giving back to his community, a gentleman who was involved in nothing, just walking down the street with his brother."

Governor Cuomo also commented how no one should have to experience the pain of losing someone they love to random gun violence. For months I could not stop crying. An unbearable pain that would not cease to subside lingered and stayed present.

The tragedy received much notoriety because of Carey being Governor Cuomo's legal assistant, but he was my husband, a caring giving man with everything to live for. We were supposed to grow old together, our hearts intertwined as one and yet he was ripped from me, from so many.

Carey earned the love and respect of all who knew him personally and professionally. He gave of himself in the prime of his life with a promising future and many attributes. Integrity, honesty, humility. He was a people person who believed in community and loved life. He was full of fun, a man who loved politics, loved to dance, and enjoyed hanging out with family and friends. A man who prayed daily and attended church weekly. He had charm, delightful to be around. He was a poet and a successful attorney.

Carey was born in the Bronx and the son of Jamaican immigrants. He graduated from Truman High School located in the Bronx Co-Op City. Growing up in a housing project, Carey could have succumbed to the violence that surrounded him. Instead, his focus was on survival and the betterment of society. To get the most out of his life by being dedicated and working hard as a student and in later life as an attorney in order to give back to and for humanity. He was the quintessential personification of the "American Dream" and his strong sense of self contributed to his success.

After high school Carey went on to graduate cum laude from Harvard, he was elected president of the undergraduate council, the main body of student government and the first black student to achieve that honor. Carey's dream was to become an attorney and his application to Harvard Law School was accepted. Following his graduation from law school, he specialized in corporate finance at several law firms in Manhattan. After leaving public finance he was devoted to the public sector and working for the state as Assistant Counsel. Subsequently, he was appointed first deputy counsel for the Empire State Development Corporation, the state's main economic development agency.

Besides Carey's brilliance, his energy, bright smile and spirit were captivating. When I met Carey I was immediately attracted to his thoughtful, kind nature. He had an inner strength that intrigued me, yet a gentle nature that made me feel secure. He was my prince charming. We dated four years, engaged one year and was only married for three.

My mother invited family and friends to meet Carey when we were engaged. As dinner was being served, Carey decided to go outside and shoot some hoops with a couple of the children who were my cousins. "What gives?" questioned my mother. I assured her it was fine and to let him have his bonding moment with them. This was indicative of Carey's kind, sensitive nature. To reach out to others and include them, particularly children.

Having children was a dream that Carey and I wanted. We had talked about starting a family, he wanted four children, and we laughed when I said that we can have two, adopt one and get a doggie. While Carey was comatose, I explored the avenues of modern medical technology as to whether we could harvest Carey's sperm. Carey was the love of my life and even though I had faith I knew that my husband was dying right before my eyes. The pain in my heart was unbearable that at one point I was even angry with him. I began to argue with him and he couldn't even respond. I then sobbed over him and I told him that his body was breaking down and that the doctors are saying that he won't make it. I shared with him what I was going to do and that was continue our dream and to try to have our baby. Before my husband died there were two things that I whispered in his ear right before the doctors took him off of life support and that was, we will receive justice and I'm going to have our child and please when you meet God, ask him to send me a healthy baby boy. Just because someone dies doesn't mean that dreams die along with them. I wanted to do everything possible to have a piece of the two of us in one and to have a breathing child to further his legacy. Gun violence killed my husband, but it was not going to kill the opportunity to have a child that would bear his name.

I am blessed that God has heard my heart cries by granting me a prayer request and I am thankful to science and the advances of medical technology that I welcomed my son, Carey Wyatt Gabay into the world on June 11, 2018.

While I suffered a tragic loss, this baby is my gift. I needed to gather all the strength I could to heal. It is gratifying to know that I have loving, supportive family and friends. But I knew that it was ultimately me who would have to take the steps to create a new meaningful existence for myself and at the time for my unborn child. As I reflected on my loss, I thought about the iniquity of the perpetrators who did this and what wickedness, darkness and immorality that had occurred in my life. I thought about what I could do to change the tragedy of my husband being a headline to a recollection of his life and how I could keep his memory alive. I sought out counseling, practiced yoga more intensely, showed up to meetings and places vulnerable and not being apologetic about it and I cried my eyes out for weeks which turned to months and then years. Those first two years were overwhelming, but I will say that those tears fueled my passion to create a new and meaningful existence which is my life and now a whole new journey of becoming a mother.

The first year that Carey passed away I decided to enter into a fast for the 9 days to acknowledge the 9 days that my husband was in a coma. It seemed like the most significant method to memorialize him and his dreams for eradicating guns violence, for justice and peace in our society. I wanted to do more to honor his memory. Carey's legacy was stellar and I wanted to continue his valuable work that would give meaning to his legacy.

Carey held the highest regard for social justice and academics. In his teens he tutored at a local community center, and succeeded academically despite his economically disadvantaged background. I established the Carey Gabay Foundation under three principles that Carey lived by, compassion, community, and integrity. My husband's life story is a testimony and serves as inspiration as a model for the foundation. As we advocate to our youth on leadership and confidence in oneself and how they can grow and flourish while realizing their maximum potential in society.

Gun violence has become rampant all across the United States. Combining Carey's love for music the Carey Gabay Foundation was inspired to host and partner with the Concert Across

America to End Gun Violence. The purpose of the concert seemed to be a meaningful fit. Our belief is that our entire nation must act as a unified collective to cease or even diminish gun violence that has escalated and senselessly claimed innocent lives, like Carey's and so many.

Consequently, the State University of New York has created the Carey Gabay Memorial scholarship program which will provide financial assistance to incoming students who exemplify the same ideals as Carey had for academic excellence, kindness and compassion for humanity.

I often at times wonder if the criminals that took my husband's life have any idea as to the devastation they have caused to our family. I was pregnant, in my third trimester as I attended my husband's trial and I looked at those men in the court room and I said to myself maybe if they had met Carey, who also grew up in a disadvantaged community, they might have been stimulated differently, but then you think of gangs and gang members who facilitate criminal activity and I wonder did they even care.

What I do know is that Carey believed in people's strengths, the will to be unified and the value for striving for a peaceful future. I am now looking to the future with promise and the new vision with our son and to show him the block in Clinton Hill where his father once lived was renamed in his honor.

My reflections about Carey are infinite. His dreams to initiate a bright future for all mankind that replace violence with diplomacy, for inclusion of various ethnic backgrounds, not exclusion. He was the role model for excellence against adversity and strife.

This will be his legacy to our society and the pride his son will inherit.

Trenelle Gabay has been an innovative icon in the fashion hair and makeup industry. While managing two salons in New York City and being a staple at fashion week, she also used her craft to give back by working in tandem with industry related philanthropic organizations, such as Locks of Love, a nonprofit which provides hairpieces to afflicted children suffering from long term medical hair loss such as cancer or alopecia areata. She also volunteered with Dress For Success, which is an organization to empower disadvantaged women to achieve economic independence. After losing her husband, Carey Gabay, to gun violence it has invariably bolstered her efforts to become an advocate for combatting social deprivation and the proliferation of guns and their misuse. In an attempt to uphold his legacy, preserve his morals and effect positive change, she founded the Carey Gabay Foundation using the same principles that Carey lived by. Compassion, integrity, and community. Since establishing the Carey Gabay Foundation she has worked alongside prominent politicians, organizations and individuals impelling change. Communing with the mayor and community leaders she incited practical revisions to the J'ouvert celebration which resulted in exponentially safer festivities. Participating in speaking circuits discussing and advocating for legislative change, and solutions to the gun violence epidemic which plagues our country. She has volunteered with "Moms Demand Action For Gun Sense in America" and she also lobbied in Washington for common sense gun legislation with the Everytown Survival Network team. Her renewed purpose is turning grievance to action, and indifference to compassion while working with people in championing solutions to create a better more sustainable environment where no one else has to endure similar tragedies.

Trenelle and Carey

Trenelle and Carey

Carey Gabay

18

NEVER AGAIN

PAUL GUTTENBERG, COMMACK, NEW YORK

"I think we have two conflicting traditions in this country. I think it's important for us to recognize that we've got a tradition of handgun ownership generally. And a lot of people — law abiding citizens use it for hunting, sportsmanship and protecting their families. We also have violence on the streets that is the result of illegal handgun usage. And so, I think there is nothing wrong with a community saying we are going to take away these illegal handguns off the streets"
~ **President Barack Obama**

"There was a shooting at Jesse and Jaime's high school today."

It was Wednesday, February 14th when I received that text from my sister in a family group chat.

At the time, I was at work and participating at a conference in South Carolina.

"Jesse is home," she continued. "They have not heard from Jaime yet."

In disbelief I replied, "Let me know when you hear anything."

I immediately panicked but did not allow myself to think of the worst. To calm myself I thought, maybe her phone was in her backpack and her backpack was still at school.

Two hours passed and still no word.

I sent another text to my sister, "any updates?"

"Not yet, Paul" she responded.

At around 6:45 p.m., as I was speaking with one of the co-workers at the conference, my sister called to tell me the news, our niece, Jaime had been shot and is dead.

Later I learned my brother Fred had spoken to a friend in Florida's law enforcement. He was an officer and had been at the scene at the Marjorie Stoneman Douglas High School.

This friend had known Jaime since she was a baby and was one of the officers to identify her dead body on the ground.

Fred and his wife, Jen had to break the news to Jesse, a junior at the high school that his sister was dead.

I kept hearing about mass shootings, but you never think you will be affected until you are. This can happen to anyone and anywhere and now it happened to me, to our family.

I sat and cried and kept thinking. How could this happen? Why did this happen?

The news of the shooting produced an unimaginable emotional upheaval. Fred and Jen's emotions were further thwarted. For two long days they were not allowed to see Jaime's body because she was part of a crime scene.

After I learned the news of the shooting, fond memories about Jaime ran through my mind. The last time I saw Jaime was the prior year, October 2017 at my brother, Michael's funeral. Michael was a first responder on 9/11 and a hero. Ultimately, he died from the toxins he was exposed to on that day.

Now, our family was faced with another tragedy. The unspeakable loss of a young child and the ravages of gun violence.

I then remembered the joyous weekend when our family celebrated Jaime's Bat Mitzvah in Florida.

My wife, Ellyn and I are Long Island residents. Our entire family traveled to Florida for this special occasion. Bar and Bat Mitzvahs have always been the main source of our family gatherings. Jaime's was one of the best. It was a weekend I shall never forget.

My niece, Jaime Guttenberg was a beautiful 14-year-old with many special attributes. She was an A student, sweet, graceful, kind with an outgoing personality. She had many friends and loved to dance. She had so much to live for but now she is dead.

At Michael's shiva, our family loudly began discussing politics as it is usual with all family gatherings.

Jaime, just being a teenager did not care to talk about politics. I remember her instead talking how she missed her dogs and looked forward to the daily snap chats she received from a friend taking care of her dogs. She loved her dogs unconditionally, the way she loved everyone in her life.

Now, Jaime will never have a sweet sixteen celebration, nor celebrate any birthday. July 13th, her birthday was always an occasion to acknowledge with joy.

I think about a whole host of things that tragically will be missed. Jaime will never get to dance again, get her driver's license, graduate high school, graduate college, attend occupational therapy school like she had dreamed of and follow in her Mom's footsteps. She will never get her first job, get married, have children or be there for family gatherings.

Now my brother and his wife start each day by visiting Jaime at the cemetery.

On February 14th, Jaime went to school to learn. At the end of that school day a killer entered her school with an AR15, a weapon of war. He hunted down and killed 17 students and teachers and wounded about 20 other innocent people.

Jaime was shot one time in the back. The velocity of the bullet was so fast that it instantly severed her spinal cord. She was dead before she hit the ground.

Jaime is survived by all her grandparents, many uncles, aunts and cousins. This event caused so much pain for Jaime's family and friends. No family should ever have to go through this. Jen, Fred and Jesse will never be fully recovered from this tragedy.

Neither will her aunt Ellyn. Nor our son, her cousin Jonathan. As Jaime's uncle, neither will I.

But I was not going to sit back and let this happen to other victims. I was going to fight and keep fighting so that the world will not forget Jaime and all other victims of senseless gun violence.

The numbers regarding mass shootings have been astronomical. It is surreal. Mass Shooting Tracker or "MST" is a site that records month by month how many people in the United States have either been injured or killed in a shooting event. The site terms "mass" shooting of four or more people.

As of July 27, 2018, 224 mass shooting events have occurred, 818 people injured by gun violence and 285 people killed were killed. I say enough! When will this madness stop?

Parkland, like Newtown, Orlando, Las Vegas and multiple others were massacres. Single deaths or massacres, any death due to gun violence is a death too many.

Our Jaime was but one among the others....each and every one of them....people like Jaime whose lives were cruelly cut short.

Blame is all over the place, like mental health, insufficient stringent background checks, and lack of safe storage. That is true. However, we must look at guns. Why does anyone need a gun, let alone a 19-year old be permitted to have an AR15?

As far as Parkland is concerned, we cannot just say the FBI and the Sheriff's Department "messed up."

While that might be true, it is ultimately the easy accessibility of guns, the National Rifle Association and the politicians who accept money from the National Rifle Association who create the environment for gun violence.

Let me be clear, while I would never own a gun, I accept the Second Amendment. However, I am opposed to assault rifles and high capacity clips. I am opposed to the NRA's leadership. I am opposed to politicians who accept money from the NRA. I am opposed to Congress not having a minute of silence after every mass shooting and "doing nothing about it."

I am opposed to hearing about mental illness and then doing nothing to help the mentally ill, and I am opposed to arming teachers but not fixing the system which failed on every level.

Don't be fooled, mass shootings can happen in any town, city or state in the United States. This is not just a Florida issue. It is an American issue. Many other countries play video games, watch violent movies and have mental illness without mass shootings. You see these mass shootings in the USA because we have the NRA, we have utter lack of gun control and we have too many guns.

I have no fear of being too repetitious but will emphasize the following: The easy accessibility of guns, no matter what their capacity and the NRA are the evil promoters for these catastrophic events and senseless deaths like our niece, Jaime.

Following the mass shooting at Stoneman Douglas High School, I spent a full week in Parkland Florida to attend Jaime's funeral. I experienced so many things that made me hopeful, so many things that made me sad and at times wanted to cry.

I was able to visit the memorials set up at the High School and at a local park for the fallen. I was able to meet many of the intelligent, articulate and brave Parkland students whose stories were captured daily on television.

Where do we go from here? WE NEED TO DO EVERYTHING.

Our society needs to be kind to those around us who are struggling. Our mental health care and social welfare systems require repair to provide the care and support for people in need.

Our schools and gathering places need careful monitoring to deter further tragedies. Our Bill of Rights needs to be protected while at the same time open to a real discussion on gun safety.

In my grief, I keep repeating to myself; SHAME ON YOU. The shame is on the National Rifle Association and those leaders in our current government who lack compassion to enact legislation to stop these senseless shootings.

However, that is just the beginning for change.

I will never stop fighting to do what I can do so that the world will not forget Jaime and all the other victims of senseless gun violence.

Since Jaime's death, I have made every effort to speak out to as many people as possible to educate people to become involved, to vote for candidates who support gun safety and to make a difference.

I am proud of the youth movement from Parkland which has ballooned all over the United States. They have taken the reins. I will follow their lead.

This generation of youth can be a guideline for raising people's consciousness to VOTE. My brother and my entire family have wholeheartedly joined them. This will be a marathon and not a sprint to work together to make our schools, malls, theaters, churches and temples safe from gun violence.

I will put pressure on the elected officials and demand change such as "Red Flag" laws passed in every state, close gun show loopholes, lobby for a stronger background check system, register all guns, increase the age to buy weapons and ban high capacity clips and weapons like the AR15.

I will wear an orange ribbon. A charity organization was formed called "ORANGE RIBBONS FOR JAIME."

The color orange was chosen because it was her favorite color. It is an energetic color, like Jaime was the picture of positive energy. It is also linked to good health and healthy foods. Jaime who was so strong and healthy.

This organization will support such causes like helping kids with special needs dealing with bullying and preventing gun violence in schools or public facilities.

"NEVER AGAIN," is not only a meaningful expression but a great movement that expresses the vital importance of saving innocent lives.

Jaime's murder is a national tragedy but for my family, it is deeply personal and unsettling.

She will be missed by the entire family and the entire family is still struggling, as well as the entire Parkland community. Many of the kids from this high school are also dealing with PTSD.

PTSD or Post Traumatic Stress Syndrome is the devastating result in the aftermath of the Parkland massacre. My hope is that our society will join me in my fight for all those students and teachers who lived through the shooting and are experiencing PTSD.

Grueling as it sounds, so many of the survivors watched classmates or teachers being shot in their classrooms and needed to step over dead bodies while leaving the building during or after the shooting.

The tragedy has left many Parkland students afraid to return to school and they will never again feel safe.

However, we are strong, we are resolute and through my partnering with this generation of the youthful activism, and Jaime's charity we will make her memory a blessing.

Paul Guttenberg and Jaime

Ellyn Guttenberg and Jaime

Jaime, Jonathan and Jesse

Jaime and Jonathan, Ellyn & Paul's son

Jaime and her dad, Fred

Jaime and Paul Guttenberg

AFTERWORD

> "When I was a student, I studied philosophy and religion. I talked about being patient. Some people say I was too hopeful, too optimistic, but you have to be optimistic just in keeping with the philosophy of non-violence."
> ~John Lewis

Contained within the preceding pages are essays written by survivors after the loss of a loved one due to gun violence. They are heart wrenching accounts of the emotional traumas experienced by the people who were personally or professionally affected.

The essays document gun violence is rampant in the United States and that guns are too easily accessible. This violence is a symptom of the turmoil our society faces today as reported daily by the media.

The compilation includes essays written by people from various walks of life and many parts of our country. Among the writers are spouses, parents, siblings, friends and clergy. The incidents include mass killings and single deaths.

All of the essayists are normal American citizens feeling alone in their tragic circumstances. Yet they are not alone in their quest for life-preserving measures regarding gun possession.

The essays undeniably confirm that regardless of who you are or where you might reside, single death of massacre, at any given moment anyone can be affected. The root cause is the easy accessibility of guns.

The common thread is that the people bravely faced their sudden, senseless tragedies, but even more importantly, counteracted their losses with valor by becoming actively involved in efforts to diminish gun violence.

Carolyn McCarthy is a sterling example of bravery and leadership to combat gun violence. After her husband and son were shot in the 1993 Long Island Railroad massacre, her congressional candidacy was initiated on this issue. Her son is still alive. but her husband died. Her service as a Congresswoman for eighteen years can be characterized as a role model in the never-ending fight against gun violence. She said:

"With my history, unfortunately with my family suffering through gun violence. it's something that I feel passionately about., that even though the odds are certainly always uphill. that doesn't mean that I will stop fighting to try to change that."

Author Lois Schaffer with Carolyn McCarthy

Gun violence can be attributed to a variety of factors. They include, the lack of restrictions on gun ownership, weak or nonexistent legislative remedies, the lack of universal background checks, lack of safe storage laws, the existence of "concealed-carry" laws, the gun-show loophole, the power and greed of the gun manufacturers and the National Rifle Association.

The preceding essays establish that gun violence has many ramifications. It is a moral, mental health, political, legislative and financial issue exacerbated by the special interest groups such as the NRA.

Effective gun safety laws can be pursued by varying means: advocacy organizations, legislation and most important, sensible legislators. There are numerous gun safety organizations. The following are illustrative of those who vigorously fight for gun safety legislation:

The Brady Campaign, Coalition to Stop Gun Violence, New Yorkers Against Gun Violence, Everytown for Gun Safety,

MOMS Demand Action for Gun Sense in America, Mayors Against Illegal Guns, Third Way and The Campaign to Keep Guns Off Campus. Each organization by various means works to educate our society, pass gun safety legislation and elect pro-gun safety legislators. In essence, these organizations emphasize social justice and their continued goal to save lives.

In 2019, I participated in the successful effort to pass Safe Storage legislation in New York State. As a survivor, a member of the non-profit organization, New Yorkers Against Gun Violence and a Nassau County resident, I was proud to join in that effort.

The bill was first introduced by Senator Liz Krueger and Assemblymember Amy Paulin. The Safe Storage bill requires that if a firearm is present in a home it must be safely stored and locked to prevent unauthorized access. Sadly, there have been instances when children have found a gun in their home, neither locked nor stored, and accidentally shoot themselves or someone else.

I contacted my Nassau County legislator, Ellen Birnbaum, for her help to enact this Safe Storage legislation. Known for her ardent concern as a legislator for social justice, her forthright actions in this regard were a source of healing and strong, positive action. Legislator Birnbaum's assistance as an advocate and elected official demonstrated the respect she has earned as a knowledgeable and devoted legislator.

From a moral perspective, how can anyone even consider such a horrendous act as willfully taking the life of another human being?

The noted author, professor and scientist, Isaac Asimov, said, "Violence is the last refuge of the incompetent."

Gun violence has often been described as a mental health issue. After a shooting, the conclusion is often reached that the killer was psychologically unstable. However, it is also true that if the gun were not readily accessible in the first place, the shooting could not have occurred.

Special interest groups such as the National Rifle Association wield enormous power. They are avaricious in the extreme and contribute mightily to the plague of gun violence by supporting legislators who are gun advocates and lobbying to pressure their resistance to all forms of gun regulation.

Mournfully, gun advocates believe that the "the only way to stop a bad guy with a gun is a good guy with a gun." The net result could be the death of both of them. The author, Oliver Markus Malloy said, "The NRA brainwashes you to believing that you need to buy a bunch of guns to protect you from all people with guns."

Time and again, this has proven to be a myth. In the August 2016, Harvard Political Review, Rachel Tropp stated, "Shootings are messy, chaotic, confusing and imperfect. Good guys with guns can't always save the day without endangering themselves or others."

"Big Guns" is a novel authored by the former Congressman, Steve Israel, from New York State. While the book can be viewed as a satire, its biting message clearly articulates congressional indifference to enacting gun safety legislation and the power of the gun lobby.

It is gratifying to note that throughout Congressman Israel's sixteen-year tenure in Washington, he fought relentlessly for sensible gun safety legislation. He received an "F" rating from the National Rifle Association....a badge of honor.

The former Congressman's voting record on gun safety legislation has been exemplary. He voted for increased federal regulation on the sale and ownership of guns. He co-sponsored a variety of bills promoting gun safety. These included: Preventing

Gun Violence Act, the Assault Weapons Ban of 2015, Background Check Completion Act, Fix Gun Checks Act 2015 and the "No Fly, No Buy Act" of 2009. This legislation prohibits any individual in possession of a gun from boarding a plane. It is interesting to note that this bill was co-sponsored by the former Congresswoman Carolyn McCarthy, whose story is also covered within these pages by Joyce Gorycki in detailing the 1993 Long Island Railroad Massacre.

Other important legislation introduced by Congressman Israel was the Undetectable Firearms Modernization Act in 2015. The legislation is an outgrowth of the Undetectable Firearms Act which passed in 1988. It is now known as "ghost guns."

With vivid clarity, I remember a meeting where the Congressman described the illicit technology for "ghost guns." They can be manufactured on a computer and can remain undetected and untraceable.

It is gratifying to note that legislation has recently been enacted addressing the "ghost guns" issue. In June 2021, three such bills were passed by the New York State legislature and signed into law in October 2021. The legislation was signed by Governor Kathy Hochul under the extraordinary leadership of Assembly Speaker Carl Heastie, Senate Majority Leader Andrea Stewart Cousins and co-sponsored by Senators Anna Kaplan, Brad Hoylman and John Brooks, Assemblymembers Chuck Lavine, Linda Rosenthal and Steve Stern.

This was just one step further to strengthen gun safety measures to save innocent lives. It has taken more than 30 years since the Undetectable Firearms Act was first sponsored to enact this legislation yet heartening that at least in New York State the scourge of "ghost guns" has been addressed. Each piece of legislation highlights different aspects of "ghost guns," their illegal construction and possession. As a whole, they lack background checks, serial numbers and are unregistered deeming them untraceable. Ultimately, they can end up in the possession of criminals making them more prone to being a public health and safety hazard.

The first of these bills is the Scott J. Beigel Unfinished Receiver Act was introduced and subsequently enacted after the Parkland massacre on February 14, 2018. That story, "NEVER AGAIN" is included within these pages. Coordinating with Senator Anna Kaplan and Assemblymember Chuck Lavine, Scott Beigel's parents, Michael and Linda Beigel Schulman, bravely tackled the issue of the illegal gun possession after their son Scott's murder at the Marjorie Stoneman Douglas High School. The legislation prohibits the sale of finished frames or receivers other than by a licensed gunsmith or firearm dealer. If the possession is discovered, it is categorized as a crime, a first or second degree felony.

The second bill is the Jose Webster Untraceable Firearms Act. It was co-sponsored by Senator Hoylman and Assemblymember Rosenthal. This law criminalizes possession of a gun that has no serial numbers.

The third bill "Disguised Gun," was co-sponsored by Senator John Brooks and Assemblymember Steve Stern. This legislation makes it illegal to disguise an actual gun to make it appear as a toy gun.

The March 2022 settlement of a civil suit by the families of victims killed in the Sandy Hook massacre was another positive step. After eight years in a legal battle, the gun manufacturer, Remington Arms agreed to a $73 million settlement for the Sandy Hook's families. Due to the Protection of Lawful Commerce in Arms Act (PLCAA) gun makers have been strongly protected against legislation. It is an historical settlement because there has never been a successful lawsuit won against a gunmaker.

While the above legislative measures and legal settlement demonstrate sensible means to save human lives, regrettably gun safety measures still remain controversial despite the efforts of the aforementioned representatives who worked tirelessly to enact gun safety legislation.

Senseless killings, America has seen a proliferation of them. They must stop.

I cannot and do not oppose all gun ownership. However, as a nation we can begin to focus on saving lives legislatively and educationally.

On a legislative level: ban assault weapons, enact universal background checks, microstamping legislation, manufacture "smart guns," eliminate the gun show loophole, repeal conceal-carry permits, expand the work of "violence interrupters," enact federal safe storage legislation and national legislation against "ghost guns."

Focusing on these gun safety measures will help limit the insidious influence of gun manufacturers and the National Rifle Association.

Educationally, create programs in schools emphasizing respect for diversity, create a national advertising program regarding the risks of gun ownership and emphasizing gun safety, allow doctors/pediatricians to talk to parents/patients about gun ownership, invest in a community based anti-violence program and create "consciousness raising" seminars for the police.

It may be unorthodox, however, but why not create a project having meetings/discussions between responsible gun owners and gun safety advocates. This kind of project could establish some common ground between those two factions and perhaps together could at least diminish the plethora of senseless killings.

However, these gun safety measures can only be enacted if there is support on the political front. We must elect candidates who will be strong gun safety advocates.

The writers represented in the foregoing pages speak for all gun violence survivors. Across the board, the underlying connections were inspirational accounts of strong, personal advocacy directed to themselves, other survivors and the nation. These writers exemplify hope and an appeal for gun safety measures to honor the loss of their loved ones and to prevent more senseless deaths.

After the Newtown massacre, Senator Chris Murphy of Connecticut said: "There is no more personal issue than gun violence, everyone of these stories is a life lost. I'm hoping that over the long term, as I tell these stories, that it will help to open people's eyes."

Not only should people's eyes be opened but so should actions be taken as the essayists who so meaningfully shared their stories in the preceding pages advocate.

It is my hope this book will inspire you to become part of the fight to bring an end to the scourge that is gun violence in the United States.

Ultimately, it is a life and death issue, and it is morally imperative.

ACKNOWLEDGMENTS

I wish to offer my heartfelt gratitude to:

Joy M. Weinberg, Managing editor, The Jewish Publication Society for her helpful assistance to create the title of this book.

Julia Wyman, formerly associated with States United to Prevent Gun Violence, who connected me with some of the essayists.

Richard Lowenstein, for his kindness and expertise in making various sections of this book more meaningful.

Ruth Karter, a dear friend, a mentor whose wisdom and guidance is most appreciated.

Debbie Heicklen, for her patience and valuable assistance with her computer skills.

My children, grandchildren and great-grandchildren, they are a source of pride and hope that they will experience meaningful, safe and healthy lives.

The Red Penguin team with special thanks to cover artist and video production by Nika Jordan Rose, editing by Janet Larkin, and book layout by JK Larkin.

Stephanie Larkin, owner and publisher of Red Penguin Books and her staff including Chris, Denise, JK, Maureen, and Nika. My infinite gratitude for her compassion and thoughtful advice. Her input to any author is a gift, including our association.

The many friends and family for their encouragement, approval and support.

David, my husband, a blend of a brilliant mind, a gentle soul, my incomparable partner and best friend.

ABOUT THE AUTHOR

Lois Schaffer has been a life long gun safety advocate. Her advocacy increased after her daughter was shot and she became a passionate activist. Given the plethora of deaths due to gun violence, she focused on this life-threatening, immoral issue and set out to identify other survivors who shared their stories about loved ones who were murdered due to illegal gun possession.

www.ingramcontent.com/pod-product-compliance
Lightning Source LLC
Chambersburg PA
CBHW060601080526
44585CB00013B/645